FIRE ANTS:

Essays Around and About Texarkana

CASON E. O'BANION

Printed in the United States of America

Please address correspondence to Permissions:

Stephen F. Austin State University Press
sfapress@sfasu.edu

ISBN: 978-1-62288-292-2

Senior Editor/Designer: Paris Taylor

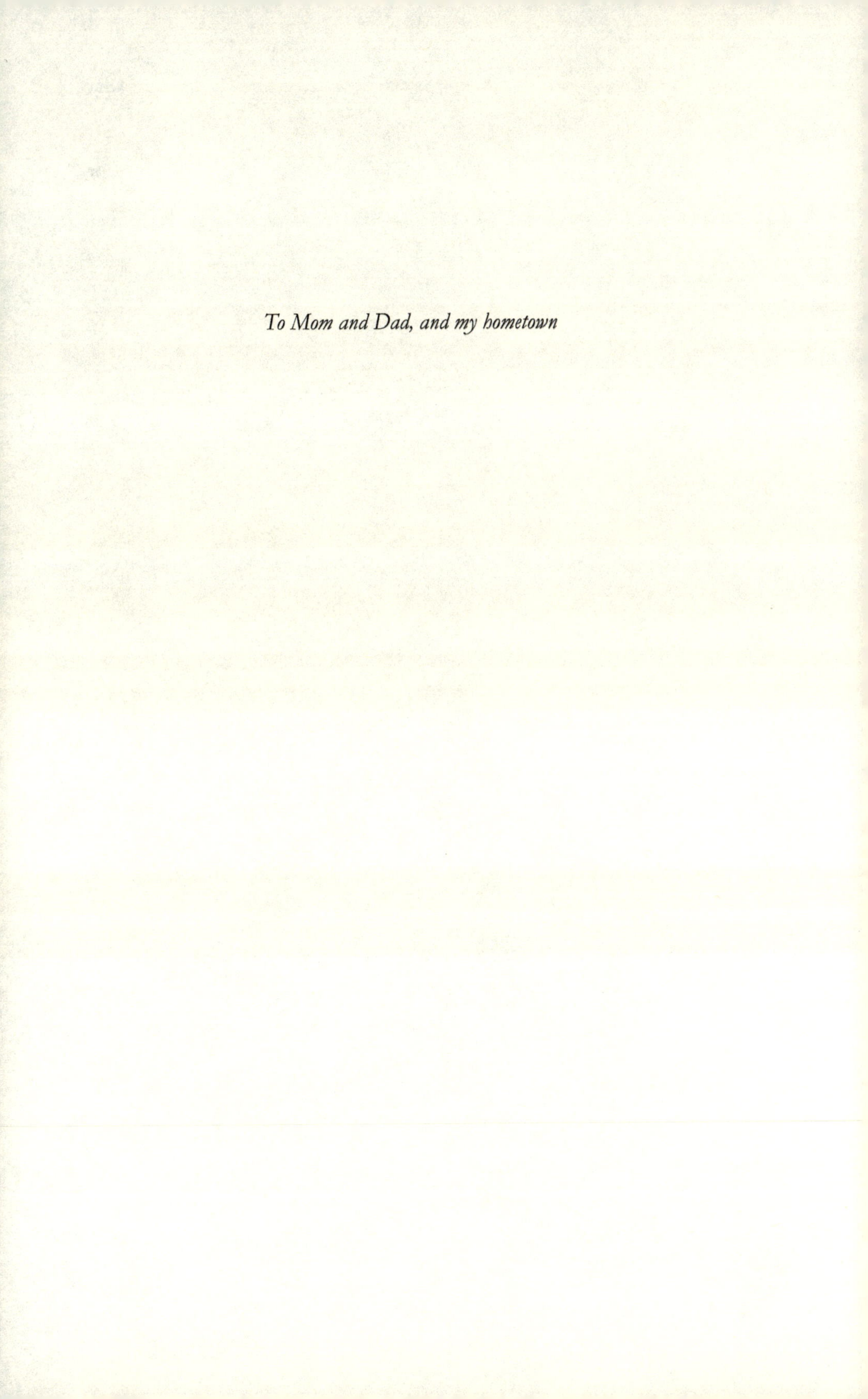

To Mom and Dad, and my hometown

CONTENTS

Introduction

As a bit of general housekeeping, the pronunciation of "Fire Ants," as shown in the title, should be in the East Texas dialect: "Far Ants." Like saying fart, but stop yourself short of the "t." Ants should be fine as is, but if you really want to get into the swing of things, try pronouncing it like "saints" without the "s." If my math is correct, you should get "Far Aints" and you're close enough to a Texarkana birth certificate.

I began these essays in graduate school in Los Angeles after my professor, the writer Jim Krusoe, admitted he was bored by the thought of reading more of the manuscript for my debut novel. About five minutes later, the dean of the program mentioned a strange encounter she'd had with a "man from nowhere—not nowhere, exactly, but someplace you'd never think of, like East Texas." I shared the first story in this collection, then another, and another, until that was all Mr. Krusoe wanted from me.

The essays in this collection are more about the inhabitants of Texarkana than their sheer Texas-ness. They, the essays, are not the Texas of oil and cattle fortunes, and in fact, some like *Amoebas* or *It's All On Ice, Alright*, could have come from anywhere and anyone that grew up through the turn of the most recent century. And yet, I find in these stories, Texas is an underlying element—never overwhelming, but there. There are more dirt bikes than horses, which I blame the cross-pollination of Arkansas culture for, mostly. We did not possess a ranch in the Texas Hill Country or an adobe near the Mexican border, but I can see it in my imagination—somewhere on the opposite end of the state. Instead, we had a lake house in a town run by a chicken-magnate—again, more Arkansas than anything. And even when setting is not a strong factor in an essay, like the two mentioned above or the one about the run of dogs at my childhood home, the events somehow spring from Texas.

Like an interaction I had recently in Lafayette, Louisiana:

"Yeah, we called all the four-wheeler flips 903ers."

A trauma nurse was staring at me, while standing at her baby shower.

During a stint in a Dallas emergency room her last year of nursing school, she'd had so many patients flown in from my hometown for either flipping ATVs, donkeys kicking out knee caps, or exploding fried turkeys, that they coined any redneck accident after Texarkana's area code: 903.

"Tried to jump his dad's lawn mower over a ditch. Fractured skull!" she called out over the baby shower crowd, mimicking an emergency room loudspeaker, a pile of blue-frosted cupcakes and once frozen, pre-grill-marked burger patties sat nearby on the linoleum kitchen counter, "903er for sure!" We laughed and almost bumped bellies before shaking our heads and staring at the gray-tile floors, reality catching up.

Four hours north of the party in Lafayette sits that scrap of Texas and Arkansas that takes shade under pine trees and spits in the eye of genealogists far and wide. Home to a population of indigenous chicken-fried steak restaurants and sulfuric well-water, the area is virtually anonymous apart from its place in the Bible Belt and state line-split post office—not near as sexy as West Texas with its postcard image of the frontier, or the hard-working, up-by-sunrise-down-by-lunch panhandle in North Texas.

Texarkana to Brownsville (at the southern-most tip) is the same distance as Texarkana to Chicago, and both in different climates. You could be in Kansas City before Amarillo. People in *the* south don't consider Texas a real southern state—although a kid I grew up with was the president of the Daughters of the Confederacy for at least one term in high school. Texans don't consider east Texas as genuine Texas. If Texas ever does secede, I imagine they'd leave the east behind. At a barber shop in 2023, I picked up a copy of Garden & Gun dubbed a deep dive into the Lone Star State—BBQ, boots, country music, tequila, hunting, cattle, and now, mysteriously, golf. Over eighty pages covering the sights, sounds, and tastes in the state and not a one on the eastern bloc. Being from Texarkana is like how I imagine living in Indiana might be, but not the part around Indianapolis or featured in Hoosiers—just the other 99%.

Once, during law school, I called my parents to tell them an adult cartoon, Archer, featured a few Texarkana references in its latest episode (it was on the interstate highway they passed while on the run). I could hear my dad's pause of disapproval at the mention of an adult cartoon. "Oh, we heard. Some Smokey and the Bandit-type show?" My mom said, "You know they came through here, right? Smokey, at least."

The origin of the town's name, a prefix orgy of Texas, Arkansas, and nearby Louisiana, is usually up for debate. The most popular theory contends that when the St. Louis Railway built its line through the area, Colonel Gus Knobel, a railroad surveyor, painted the name on a plank and nailed it to a tree. "This," he proclaimed, "is the name of a town which is to be built here." A local college coined their mascot after the train. My favorite stems from the legend that bank and train bandits hid in the unincorporated woods, so the two states split it down the middle in an execution of justice—it adds a touch of excitement, like an orphan assigning themselves some fantastic lineage.

An old professor of mine in Los Angeles mistakenly mis-pronounced Texarkana every time, subliminally assuming elegance in the vacancy of sophistication. She called it "Tex-ar-cohn-ah," like it belongs to a tribe of native nobility.

"It's pronounced Texar-KAN-uh," I say back. "An, not on. You can't forget about the Arkansas in there."

My brother lives in Atlanta, Georgia, now, next to the actors Owen and Luke Wilson—both from Dallas. Talking one night over a dog bite situation on their street, Owen told him he remembered Texarkana well and had driven through it many times as a kid. "I enjoyed Tex-ar-cohn-ah," he'd said. It must be a Los Angeles thing.

It's not that fancy, guys. REM got it right in their song, Texarkana. Modest Mouse got it right. American Psycho got it right, too— the name Texarkana written in lasso rope stretched across the big screen in theaters nationwide—even if it was the country-western restaurant Patrick Bateman settled on after multiple rejections at Dorsia.

ꝏ

When you're from a small town, you find anything to latch onto for shreds of notoriety or slivers of context in conversations in airport lounges or cross-country Zoom calls.

A buddy from work, originally from Pascagoula, Mississippi—a town I only knew from an old VHS comedy tape my parents played on road trips about a squirrel that went to church and shocked a bunch of Baptists—was telling our office about Pascagoula's most famous son, Jimmy Buffett, who was born there on Christmas day right after World War II. Another coworker broke in, this one from New Orleans, and explained that Buffett graduated from high school in Mobile, so that meant he was actually *from*

Mobile. I shook my head—at both the Jimmy Buffett conversation and incorrect origin assessment. Small towns like Texarkana and Pascagoula need not apologize for wielding some flexibility when claiming celebrity relation. Cities like New Orleans, on the other hand, should only certify someone born and raised within their municipal limits. Reese Witherspoon was born in New Orleans but went to middle school in Tennessee. She's from Tennessee. Ellen DeGeneres was born and raised in New Orleans… almost. She moved to Atlanta, Texas when she was fifteen and completed high school with her mom and, by all accounts, horrific stepfather. My dad can make it to Atlanta in twelve minutes if he's "lettin' the engine eat," as he says, so Ellen is, in many ways, from Texarkana. She ran from the area soon after high school graduation and probably hasn't been back, but thanks for stopping by.

On a road trip with my brother in 2010, we went through a town in Nevada on our Garmin GPS Map. Straight through it. We'd been driving for hours in the desert night, lit up by the stars and moon–no neon gas stations. David's 2003 trailblazer was packed to the brim, every belonging that he could see fit to bring to Portland, Oregon, for his medical residency – clothes, frisbees, a handstitched picture of conquistadors. The seats had to lean about 5° forward more than you'd want, like a stewardess was going to catch you if you got comfortable. Our bags served as a formidable privacy curtain on the center console.

"Only thirty more miles," David said. "Stay awake! Stay awake—they have a hotel and a Mom-and-Pop sandwich place I saw on the map." Mom and Pop was now part of his Portland vernacular.

I'd been shouted down from ordering a WhataBurger only the day before.

The wind blew so hard that the RPM hand jumped back-and-forth based on how big the 18-wheeler was in front of us. We drafted from truck to truck like an F1 driver on a straight away, only we were dodging stray cactus fronds, not concrete barriers.

With only a few gallons left in our tank, we finally got to the spot on the map—Carson, not Carson City, just Carson—and the fuzzy map blinked in the darkness of the car before our little blue truck jolted over the dot.

I took down the bag barrier as the dot faded on the map and the image of more cacti and coyotes appeared around the digital interstate, our blue toy truck hitching forward down the road.

"What was that?" I asked.

"I guess," David said, seeming to weigh the options of running out of gas and suing Garmin, "I guess that town just doesn't exist? I don't know."

There was no exit, no lights, no gas station, no Mom or Pop.

We found an old casino hotel an hour later and had a delicious Whopper when our Trailblazer growled into Tonopah, NV in the midst of a biker rally festival. We'd skipped the Clown Inn—a motel with clown figurines in every room—which I assumed we'd be gruesomely and unceremoniously murdered in, which might've been preferable to the coin operated air conditioning window unit in the casino hotel.

A large biker in a leather vest stumbled onto the caged elevator with us around midnight, asking if we were there for the rally. Me in Birkenstocks and my brother in either scrubs or one of his many colorful guayabera shirts he insisted I squeeze into a few times throughout the trip, didn't feel a need to answer but asked him about Carson, NV and it's sudden disappearance.

"Oh, yeah. Everybody done forgot about that place when the interstate went around it. Even the people who lived there forgot they were from there."

I would say most small towns are trying to avoid the obscurity looming with an interstate bypass.

Texarkana doesn't have any fruit or known exports to stake a claim to. That might not be a problem for most of the country but being so close to Louisiana where every parish is the capital of the world for *something*. My mom grew up in Ruston, Louisiana, which, according to the billboards outside of town, is the peach capital of the world. She was Princess Peach in the annual Peach Festival. I had friends in college from Rayne, Louisiana—the frog capital of the world. Des Alamedas, Louisiana became the catfish capital of the world in the 1970s until the Mississippi governor unilaterally gave the title to Belzoni, Mississippi. The following year, the Louisiana legislator, not to be outdone and focusing on the important topics of the 1980s, declared Des Alamedas the Catfish Capital of the Universe—squashing any cultural relevancy that Belzoni might hope for within the Virgo Supercluster. Breaux Bridge is the crawfish capital of the world. Mamou, a town I remember best for a Mardi Gras parade which included men on horseback in white hoods that politely encouraged spectators to drink from a jug of who knows what that tasted like equal parts Tabasco, tire fire, and honeysuckle, while kids chased a greased pig and chicken around the town square, chose the Cajun music capital of the world. If you haven't heard Cajun zydeco music—imagine if elevator music didn't graduate from middle school. I did some work in my 30's in Washington Parish, Louisiana, which, until a coworker had a birthday party for his one-year-old daughter themed One in a Melon, I had no way of knowing was the watermelon capital of the world. I should've known based on the roadside stands selling watermelons as big as my four-door sedan: green, yellow, red, seedless, seeds shaped like torsos, others like dachshunds.

Texarkana doesn't have something as polarizing as a watermelon, a strawberry, a crawfish, a frog, or even the dogtrot like Dubach, Louisiana, but one of the first viral YouTube videos was filmed in the woods behind my high school—a black and white scene of a kid discussing Chic-Fil-A, our mall's arcade, and Dr. Zhivago with crunched leaves and twigs providing the soundtrack.

We had some professional athletes and musicians, specifically the Christian rock variety. One guy—Scott Joplin—popularized ragtime in the early 20th century, and his piano is still in downtown Texarkana today. Ragtime spun itself into jazz somewhere along I-49 on the way to New Orleans. A more creative mind than myself might assert that Texarkana, possibly, in some way shape or form, founded jazz. New Orleans people won't like that. But I have no reason not to believe the tour I went on in 3rd grade.

And sure, Texarkana is known for being in two states at once. I'd soon learn that a few places were in multiple states, so that's nothing to hang your hat on. We had a zoo, an outdoor habitat showcasing wildlife particular to the area, but it had to be shut down after hunters poached all the white tail deer. I watched Donald Trump Jr. desperately impersonate a Texarkana native in an interview recently, decked out in camo and waving some kind of scoped gun above his head, talking about states' rights. I've often loathed friends who act as if being from *their* hometown is the only place to be from, but I've come to see hating your hometown as even worse. Something tells me the Remington in Don Jr.'s hand wasn't the same caliber as the one Remington Browning Savage, a kid on my Dixie Youth baseball team, used on his morning hunts before class our junior year. Not to paint by number too much, but Remington, Browning, and Savage are all gun brands. It was a mystery, then, when he got kicked out of school for leaving a shotgun in his truck after a duck hunt.

We were on the history channel for some kind of boggy creek monster. The local baseball umpire and a Little Debbie delivery man were interviewed about the validity of the monster, which they neither confirmed nor denied. Instead, the Little Debbie delivery man prattled on about the supposed health benefits of oatmeal cream pies.

The town is the inspiration behind the Texas Chainsaw Massacre, based on a series of murders in the early 20th century. But the house where the murders supposedly took place has since been steamrolled for a strip mall that included not one, but two Burlington Coat Factory outlets. I'd heard more than once that the woman that murdered Selena was from

Texarkana, but she wasn't.

Schools have generic mascots.

Without a big ball of yarn or a famous cuisine, it's difficult to pinpoint not where you're from but what you come from. I want to say Dallas but people from Dallas don't deserve a ridiculous city christening origin story. I'll use Shreveport as a landmark, but the casinos and bars open past ten p.m. are far beyond the comprehension of the Texarkana protestant population. Little Rock wants to be Dallas and their airport has more than one terminal, so that won't work. Someone asked me recently if I grew up near Beaumont. Nobody had ever conflated east Texas to Beaumont, which is clearly southeast Texas, born of the sediment of western Louisiana—those Houston offshoots crawling out of the Gulf and into their Shipley's Donuts.

"No, Jesus Christ," I said.

"Then what's near Texarkana?"

"I don't know," I said. "Paris, Texas; Atlanta, Texas; Pittsburg, Texas; a Boston that they call New Boston." There's a Lake Palestine, too, but you pronounce it Pal-Eh-Steen.

An area void of the creative juices needed for naming a municipality, Texarkana is easy to find on a map in Bowie County—named after the knife, of course, not the pop star. We have that and Applebee's. And People.

The people that make up the area are the basis for these and many other stories. There's my friend Tyler with two different NASCAR-themed tattoos, both on his ass. When Tyler read one essay about him, he called me to tell me he loved me, and he was excited to get my debut novel that came out a few weeks later. I reminded him it was fiction, saying it wasn't real unlike the essay. "Shit, I know what fiction is," he said, "It's like Hank the Cowdog stuff." There's Patrick, who could've gone to Oxford but wanted to try door-to-door popcorn sales instead. There's Edward, John David, Cody, Hunter, Matthew, Austin, Tommy, Brian, Jonathan, and Clint, and beauty queens fighting with foreign exchange students watching—and others with stories and lives that intersect around and outside the interstate system that carves through the area. Then there are those that make it run—the Tysons and the McGuires and the Maddoxs—whose lives of generosity and kindness transform the tolerable into downright cozy. And teachers like Mr. Kirk, Mrs. Campbell, Mrs. Copeland, and Mrs. Harris who are devoted to public schools like I never could be. Not as many wild stories, just lives well-lived and legacies born out of genuine appreciation and the sediment of the Red River—in many ways more interesting than Johnny Cash stopping through town on his debut tour or a band of robbers hiding out in an untamed, unnamed forest.

Then of course there's me. After I left for college in 2007, my trips home became less frequent. What was once a great opportunity to go out with old friends has turned into choosing to watch movies with my kids at my parents' house, or bypassing Texarkana, absconding to the lake house in nearby Pittsburg, Texas. What might come through in these essays is a genuine, in a protestant preacher sort of way, feeling that I don't know what living there is like, but I do know how idyllic growing up there could be and was at one point. It was hot in the summers but still snowed in the winter, the schools were rivals but friends, the restaurants were Chili's and Olive Garden but those rock anyway, and my friends and I, and everyone it seemed, got into a lot of trouble but somehow none at the same time. These essays don't cover everything about me and my time in Texarkana. They can't. I don't know if I even mention showing my kids the exact spot in my parents' laundry room I got caught making out with my girlfriend (my now wife and their mom) after my oldest sister's wedding.

I am of course reminded while writing these that this is one side of a geographically and culturally divided town. Essays like the one about my friend Andre, where I try to guess at what it must've felt like to be one the handful of black kids in a white-flight school system from kindergarten through senior year—balancing friendships, rides, and schoolwork on imaginary lines drawn well before even your parents were born—are an attempt at good faith recognition to the other side of the proverbial tracks but often and most definitely fall short of telling the full story of Texarkana. Instead, these essays account my version of events, my perspective, my friends, which includes Andre and a host of people from different walks of life. I hope they feel adequately represented and respected. I know how beautiful it was for me to grow up there and looking back brings a smile to my face, but that isn't the same for everyone.

I am proud to be a 903er—myself having flipped a four-wheeler in the snow on Christmas Break in 2001.

FIRE ANTS:

Essays Around and About Texarkana

All-Star Special

I asked my dad how he was warming up to his potential son-in-law once. The guy, who'd been dating my sister for a couple of years, was coming off a particularly embarrassing performance on Texarkana Country Club's golf course. "Well," my dad said, "he's not much of a golfer, but neither are you. He's smart, but how good a school is Notre Dame, really? I don't know, just not the type you'd want next to you inna scrap at Waffle House. It wont last."

And it didn't. The guy used the money he'd saved for an engagement ring on a trip to Bhutan, where, to my knowledge, there are no Waffle Houses.

ꝏ

Years before, in high school, a group of us sat in the cab of my friend Austin's newfangled, Midnight Black 2005 Tahoe. It was silent, except for the rhythmic beat of packing dip cans. It was late July, right before our senior year, and we'd had the freedom to get off work and "shit around," as my dad put it, until loose curfew calls came later. Most of us worked at the supermarket as baggers, checkers, or stockers (I, myself, was a cake decorator in the bakery and invented a spider cake Albertson's Grocery still uses to this day and hasn't paid a royalty dime for). Others dug sand traps at golf courses, bussed tables at restaurants, or performed other odd jobs in the air conditioning, something my dad wouldn't allow before this very summer, and I choose to spend it hunched over an oven. We had some newfound independence after work, the shitting around time, except for Collin—he'd shot his neighbor's dog, believing it to be a coyote, so he had to go straight home from his court-ordered community service at the kill-kennel each night. He was a crack shot and would perform well in Afghanistan years later.

Outside was a still, soupy mess. The humidity coated the windows of the car, but inside the cabin of a Tahoe was as close to luxury as some of us could hope for apart from the Tour of Italy plate at the Olive Garden across town.

"So, you see," my friend Tyler said, "Cheeseburger's pissed, as any of us would be, because Cash has been texting Brittney. And y'all just know that idiot is willing to stand up for her for no damn reason." Tyler was a rail of a kid, 6'1 with a mop of dusty brown hair dragging along his neckline, sideburns stretching to mid-jaw. Stuffing a pinch of brown dip deep into his gums, Tyler spit out more of the backstory as Austin, Daniel, and myself nodded.

A noon, noon-thirty text each summer day would lay out our options each night—maybe a party in a field, someone's parents were out of town, a band was playing at the old bar that didn't card us, or on the special nights, there was a fight.

"Who is Cash again?" I asked.

"He's a big ol'boy from the Arkansas side. Or Red Lick. I don't remember, but he's got a different area code. I saw the messages."

"Has Cheeseburger ever been in a fight?"

"Hell no," Tyler laughed. "'Cept with his dad, maybe. Can't imagine it went well either way."

"And how does Brittney know Cash?" It turned out that Cash and Brittney worked together at The Movie Gallery video store.

Cheeseburger was a scrawny kid, malnourished in the way that gives you a small paunch belly, and he was standing at the center of a freshly paved asphalt parking lot, his hair matted to his forehead, combed down and straight across like he had gotten it cut at Auto Zone. A small stud earring reflected our headlights and a damp gray t-shirt sat on his shaking shoulders. His real name was Matt, not Matthew, Matt, but he had a large grayish brown birth mark on his arm in the shape of a cheeseburger, so his older brothers always introduced him a such.

The Texas side's Applebee's was the second highest grossing location in the entire country for two years straight, largely due to the commercial interstate travelers from Dallas and Little Rock, and the all-night breakfast spot across the street benefitted from any stragglers. Hosting fights here added to the air of low-grade violence about town. The yellow glow of the Waffle House marquee pooled warmly on the windshields of the cars, its glare dancing off an aluminum baseball bat in Cheeseburger's left hand.

"What the hell did Cheeseburger bring a bat for?" Daniel asked, his dark arms wrapped around the front passenger headrest, face peering out from above. That bat had to be from the Dixie Youth Baseball team we had been on for years, and he was a disaster with it then. We didn't have Little League in Texarkana, but we did have Dixie Youth—complete with a small rebel flag logo on the sleeves.

A blue truck rumbled into the lot, spitting fumes from its rusted exhaust onto the sidewalk hedge. With its overhead lights full throttle and its music vibrating the loose passenger door, the body of the truck teetered on four-foot lifts, or at least high enough I could see the yellow springs spiraling up from the muddy wheels.

"Arkansas side," Austin said. Saliva and tobacco drooped from his mouth onto the lip of a punched-out Coke can. Austin and Daniel were two of the best soccer players in the city, but both played with a small pinch of tobacco in-between their toes. Austin claimed it kept him calm, but it surely aided in him losing his college soccer scholarship years later. He was big, and I'd seen him in a few scraps and fights, mixing it up with the best of them.

The blue truck swung into a parking spot and almost up on the curb.

There's a moment when a firecracker's fuse sucks into the cylinder, right before it hits the powder. The crackle of flames goes out and for a split-second, everyone wonders if it's a dud. Then, if it's a reputable brand like Black Cat, it explodes.

The truck's passenger door rattled to a halt, the exhaust stopped shaking, and the music shut off for split-second before the four doors flung open, and five grown men in oil-stained blue jeans hopped down from the creaking running boards. The kids from the Arkansas side had a way of looking like they'd just put in a double shift at the tire factory on their side of town, and in that way, they always looked more like men than the boys we'd grown up with.

Cheeseburger started shouting, "Hey! Hey now!" with one foot backing away, the other planted firm on the asphalt.

"Damn," I said, and I felt a nervous smile stretch across my face. I loved watching fights; I think everybody does. I'd watch them in college the next year, and I'd watch them in New Orleans in my adulthood—none of them sanctioned by anything but a loose mob. But there's a tinge of fear you feel for the underdog. It's a distressing pity when you know someone is about to be physically reprimanded by a peer, especially in public. College bar fights have an air of spontaneity. Someone brushes into someone else, words are exchanged, and it starts. Hell, I accidentally bumped a man's arm last week at my kids' church preschool fundraiser auction while he was raising a spoon on gumbo to his mouth, and he turned like it might be on. These high school fights were planned meetups. There was time for anticipation and a crowd to build, and there were more than a few cars in that Waffle House parking lot that had backed into their spot, headlights on but low.

All I could think about was Cheeseburger running a fifteen-minute mile the year before in gym class, and him being the perennial first-out in dodgeball every week.

"Y'all," I leaned forward from the back, elbow on the center console. "Is Cheeseburger about to die?"

"Well, if he does," Tyler said, "it'll be for the dumbest reason I've ever heard. Brittney's not even here."

"Roll the windows down!" Daniel shouted.

A semi-circle formed in front of Cheeseburger, most of them wearing t-shirts, patched greenish brown camo, all of them in brown leather, square-toe boots that looked more worn-in than the black ostrich skin pair Tyler got after his parents traded in the family's Bowflex stock.

"Cheeseburger, you stupid sack a'shit," a man in the front said, eyes hidden under the shade of a V-shaped denim baseball cap bill. "She was talkin' to me an' I just talk back."

"Don't, don't try to get out of this, Cash," Cheeseburger said, fist balled, face sweating. "You, you knew she was with me."

"What'd ya brung a bat for, ya stupid shithead?"

"In case you brought friends."

"Ya got a tee-ball game later?"

"Cash, Cash... We don't have to do this."

"I sure didn't drive all the way up here to talk, buddy," Cash said, hooking his index finger into his lip and pulling out a fat, soggy lump, throwing it on the ground. "Les fuckin' go."

"Get away from my car with that bat, Cheese!" Austin was leaning out his window, glaring at the five feet in between Cheeseburger and the Tahoe's headlights.

"Austin?" Cheeseburger spun around. "What the hell you doin' here, man? Guys?" I could see the desperation in his eyes then. The headlights brightening the vulnerable angles of his face. "Get out and HE-lp!" His voice cracked, and it was all over.

"Run, Cheese!" we shouted as he turned. He flung the bat forward like a fencer and it dropped to the ground, the clang of aluminum rang out as Cheeseburger's arms flailed. "Cash!" he wailed, in a clunky dead sprint. "Cash, I'm so sorry!"

The Arkansan guys followed, one stopping to retrieve the bat. Work boots pounded on the pavement, whoops and frantic hollers filled the night as the crowd headed toward the darkness of the back lot. Cheeseburger might be dead meat, but he was no fool—if he could run far enough and they kicked his ass across the state line in Arkansas, it would technically be a felony.

The stench of exquisitely cooked waffles and burnt eggs wafted from an open door, the night manager filling the frame and screaming for the group to "Git!"

"Did y'all know the Gulf War wasn't anywhere close to the Gulf of Mexico?" Tyler broke in, as we pulled out of the parking lot in search of the next food fight.

Just a couple of weeks ago, I took my wife and kids to a special Valentine's dinner at a white table-clothed Waffle House in Baton Rouge, Louisiana. I'd seen hookers, pimps, pirates (from the Port of Call pirate bar next door that burned down in 2021), and drunks gathering at this exact location since college. "You did ya'self good to-nigh, baby," the pimp had said. "Three-fitty. Woo-wee. Ya thas good. Get them chocolate chips in your waffle."

I felt the same telling my four-year-old daughter that, a pile of red roses crunching under our milks and coffees. The hostess and staff were all in prom gowns, running back and forth while a cartoonist offered to draw our picture under the haze from the pink light bulbs and scorched hash browns. They brought the waffles out, but with the chocolate chips *on top* of Flan's waffles. I told her this wasn't the 24-hour diner experience I'd known and loved. But as she poured double the FDA recommended yearly dosage of syrup for Andre The Giant onto her warm plate, the chocolate mixed and melted into the maple and butter to create a swirl of deep, sweet soil. She took a bite, somehow covering her nose and eyelids in the sauce, and she smiled.

Laziness fosters all invention in this southern shark tank. And they always hit it big.

It's All On Ice, Alright

"Hey, Melissa, good morning, um, you may or may not listen to this message, but I was just saying hi, and did you ever think of a gift card idea for Casey—this is going to be kind of a gift card Christmas for the grown-ups, like, I have some ideas for others, like for example James, I gave him a gift card to Specs because he likes to drink, and David, I think I'm giving him a big gift card because he won't buy anything big for himself, you know, so maybe to some hipster cool store that I've never even heard about, and Mary Claire suggested this cool golf store place for Brent's—it's like an online golf store I think, so perfect for a gift card anyway. I just can't think of really anything for Casey. If you had an idea that would be great, helpful, whatever if you don't—I'll just come up with something. O-kay. I hope you're having a good day. I'm kind of having a whiplash day coming home from the lake and Katie's, and I'm trying to get my things in order because Katie is bringing her kids tomorrow, so I'm kind of losing the weekend anyway. All good. It's all good. Big tree on the house from the storm, but, you know, other than that everything is pretty great here. O-Kay, I will just, just… think maybe nothing too exotic but somewhere Casey would like to spend a gift card—it's not that personal of a gift, I guess, but you get the point – just something fun and unique to the person. I don't need another scene. What's something he would enjoy using but it's basic enough to even have a gift card because, you know, a lot of places don't even have gift cards like that little coffee shop he likes, I'm sure they're too cool for a gift card, but would he drink Starbucks if I gave it to him? I doubt he cares much. I didn't even know he drank coffee, to be honest. Oh, well. I'm looking out the kitchen window at this pine on the garage. It's huge—*hugh-mun-gous*. Missed the Ferrari though or else Dennis would have just died. Texarkana made the National Weather Channel last night, so big day today. What else do you want for Christmas? Anything to eat? I could do Charlotte Russe but probably not time for that! Making the gumbo here. Hope the TSA is in a good mood when we go through security. They thought I was crazy bringing frozen trout in our carry-ons last time – Dennis said we should check them, but I thought that might be suspicious. Not in a hijack-y sort of way, but just in a who brings frozen trout on an airplane sort of way. Really. If you didn't know Dennis, you'd think he was still an 18-wheeler driver. All he wants are new compression socks for Christmas, so I got him the kind Brett Favre is always modeling on T.V. He's worried the beer he's going to leave out for the garbage men will freeze since it's going to be, you know, below freezing. I told him, *Dennis, you can give them beer another time*, or they can probably get their own beer, but he loves doing that, so he rigged some system out there to keep the beer warm enough so it won't freeze, and they can have it Christmas Day. He calls it "rodeo cold" because that's how they serve them at rodeos, like he's ever been to a rodeo. The dogs are chasing the neighbor, I can see them from the window. Daisy! No! O-Kay, all right, all right, I have to run. Thanks, bye…"

Fire Ants

People used to ask me how *big* Texarkana was, and I think they meant how many people lived there. That answer is something around eighty thousand in the surrounding areas, maybe more, but the real answer is that it wouldn't look out of place if a four-wheeler were driving through a major intersection.

I haven't been back much lately—when you're thirty-two in the south, weddings, the good ones at least, are long gone—but I'd imagine there's one street legal dirt bike to every Tesla up there. I'm probably underestimating my hometown, and overestimating Tesla—driverless dirt bikes never killed anyone. It was a place, secluded by a two-hour drive to any major city, where the cop that pulled you over might be your middle school DARE officer, and where you knew someone every time you went to Target. Inside the boundaries of the singular zip code sat an ecosystem of rich, poor, middle class, and the bourgeoise of the American rubber tire, chicken, and trucking industries. I remember going to a Y2K party at a house with a rundown tennis court, its tattered net hanging by a nylon string—trucking family.

It was an easy place to grow up, but an inexplicitly difficult place to leave despite recently developed accessibility to the two interstates. I have a tolerance, bordering on admiration, for the place's limits.

Something happened to Texarkana kids around puberty—they'd go through the normal rigmarole of maturation, but the boys, mostly, would grow deeper voices and a palpable twang. As for me, I attempted to ditch any accent during my senior year when I went for a college visit and everyone was laughing at a kid from Dallas—a kid I thought sounded more like Frasier Crane than Beverly Hillbilly. In south Louisiana, where the kaleidoscope of drawls, hitches, and slurs spin anyone into a real headache, the slow but sharp punch of an east Texas-southern Arkansas accent was too much for the locals. I've come to define it by the way you choose to pronounce "y'all" – if you add a "w" behind the "a" and stretch the word for two seconds, you're in the ballpark. If you're ever yelling it across a packed Texas Roadhouse dining room when you see a friend walk in the double doors, feet crunching the peanut shells – you're there.

With the thicker accent came other customary accoutrement: more convincing camo hanging in the closet, larger tires on the truck (which you should park at the edge of the driveway for clear visibility), fishing gear, and a circular impression of minty mouth tobacco carved into your blue jeans. I wasn't destined for any of these sacred rights: I went hunting three times before high school, all with my dad, who enjoyed sitting around the fire, encircled by friends and camper trailers, more than the actual hunt itself. I fell in some icy water the first time, the time my MaMere told me she'd pray we didn't shoot any ducks on account of their beauty and how poorly they were cooked "up here." She was from New Orleans and never stifled a giggle any time my north Louisiana dad put something on the table. I stayed on the four-wheeler that day and cried; my hand-me-down waders filled with not-quite-hypothermic inducing water. Another time I shot an eight-point buck and enjoyed a rare high-five from my dad. Then the last I sat alone, pretending to enjoy a book before doing something I'd rather not mention – I never fired the *actual* gun that time. The shaking stand surely warded off any deer. I haven't been since the invention of cell phones, but I'd imagine shooting both to be more accessible.

Besides hunting, I had a used Japanese brand SUV that I didn't think tires would look great on, fishing was fun but not as much as not fishing, and I watched as six of my friends tried dip for the first time in ninth grade in a poorly lit backyard—all of them puking in the flower bushes about fifteen minutes later. I wimped out there.

Others avoided it, too. My friend Edward casually deflected any tobacco offers, drove a mid-sized sedan, and, since his parents were from Houston, had the air of the big city around him, which meant he listened to and knew about rap. It wasn't until years later I learned Edward went to the only private school in town up to seventh grade. I didn't find out he'd gone there, but that it was private.

Edward's little brother Clayton Hill really ran with the changes. First, my dad took him hunting a few times to show him the ropes. Then Clay got a truck, a drawl, and a particular brand of spit tobacco.

Home from law school years later, my dad took me around our yard to kill fire ant beds. He yelled at me from across the lawn to stop messing around and just "kick the shit out of 'em." That was the best way to do it—just run up and kick the ant pile, scattering their interstates, families, and entire way of life across layers of pine needles and gravel driveways. He looked down and somber while we went about our kicking, the same way I'd seem him play with the rubble of his childhood home after new owners bulldozed it for the pecan prospects—his feet dribbling dark asphalt like a soccer ball when he told us how long his dad had saved up to get that driveway put in. When we finished with the ants, he told me Clay had died—a gun accident in his apartment.

A few, a brave few, commemorated the event by getting guns tattooed on their chests or arms. Rifles on biceps, machine guns with his initials down the barrel on chests. One got it on his back.

That was Tyler.

Tyler never had any social media, so he didn't know that modern acceptable grief came with a changed profile picture or quick anecdote discussing how hard *you've* been affected. A tattoo, his body is now covered in them, was his quickest way of saying I'll miss you. His other tattoos (most notably Dale Earnhardt Jr.'s Budweiser-sponsored red number eight across his left butt cheek, which he had to modify to include a green eight once "Junior," as Tyler called him, changed his sponsor to Mountain Dew and his number to eighty-eight) mostly ran up his arms. A rail-thin, tan kid with stringy brown hair, Tyler personified the puberty shuffle inundating our group of friends. Once focused on sports—a team picture from our refrigerator comes to mind with Tyler, a shaved-headed ten-year-old with a wild look in his eyes kneeling in front of a soccer ball, blue jersey stretched around his small but sturdy frame, his hand clenching his boney kneecap—he moved into high school and onto other vices.

Any part of Tyler that didn't scream redneck was most likely some window into his upbringing, a hint that his family had quite a bit of Bow Flex stock and sold it around the time it meant something to sell quite a bit of Bow Flex stock. His parents divorced when we were young, and his mom married the country club's golf pro a few years after. His dad did something I didn't and still don't quite understand, but he owned a hunting camp on the side, one with zebras and buffaloes somewhere in east Texas, where we met people like Dallas Cowboys owner Jerry Jones. I met the lead singer of a band called the Eagles there once. I'd just tried my first joint, masturbated in a bathroom with deer antlers hanging over the mirror and holding the toilet paper, and walked out to shake hands with Don Henley. I watched a documentary about The Eagles a few years back with my dad. He'd met

Henley once and remarked about how rude he was during the process. I told my dad about my experience with him, and we laughed—we couldn't bond over hunting, but we both hated the Eagles.

Another thing that came along with hunting, fishing, dip, and the Texarkana speech impediment was drinking. We mainly did it at a friend's house, grabbing what we could when we could. One night, I grabbed an old bottle of champagne and ran to my Japanese SUV, speeding off down the road. We pulled swigs until the label was clear, and I could see it was definitely from my parents' wedding night in 1979. Tyler drove me home that night in his American brand truck.

Tyler is the type of person I've always been infatuated with—someone who has accomplished almost nothing but could have accomplished almost anything. For a while, his greatest claim to fame was the only kid to ever win student body president from ISS (In School Suspension). No campaign posters, no empty promises—just the image of Tyler raking donuts with his truck tires before a varsity football game to sway the vote. We'd drank before the first game of our senior year, painted our faces, and sprayed enough body spray down our shirts to give an elephant asthma—masking the smell of alcohol with scents like *Masculine Musk*, *Provocation*, and *Wild Instinct.* Tyler took his truck and did a few donuts in the stadium parking lot. I can still hear the ping of his truck nuts swaying on his trailer-hitch, slapping his bumper and shimmering amidst the spray of dirt and gravel for a brief moment in time before wobbling still when the truck stopped—our DARE officer had pulled up with the assistant principal and caught him. He had a thirty-pack of beer in his truck bed, which looking back on it, makes me wonder why they're sold in such high quantity. He won in a landslide but ruled the meetings via notes he scribbled from the corner of the white cinderblock classroom at the back of the Annex building. I told him years later that, since the truck wasn't born a man, adding the nuts might be seen as a pretty progressive move on his part—especially in the trans community. Tyler laughed, "I need all the friends I can get," he'd said.

I served two short stints in ISS that year, once with the class treasurer and vice president, which, with me as the class secretary, made the entire governing body of Pleasant Grove's Senior High out to lunch that day.

When his dad learned about the beer, ISS, and drunk donuts, he took Tyler to the federal prison up the road to show him what life was like inside. His dad's friend, the warden, took Tyler to meet two men that had recently bound and gagged the local Outback's wait staff before robbing and murdering them. Tyler claims he cried but judging by the ample other drunk donuts I've seen him pull, I can't say it worked. Now that I have a son with what I'd call an almost predisposed inclination for chugging Capri Sun in less than a second, I've re-opened the dialogue on this experiment.

ꝏ

I don't remember anyone ever saying no to Tyler. He had that way of speaking to you like he was really listening, because he was. No distractions, no cell phone clicking, no interruptions—just a crooked smile and the God's honest truth.

He graduated in the middle of our 120-person class with no college aspirations despite the grades and money to try. He was once the Accelerated Reader points champ in sixth grade—a public school initiative where each book was assigned a certain point value and students had to read and pass a quiz to reach the mandatory mark each six week term. It was meant to boost reading and comprehension but probably increased literature film adaptation as complimentary side effect. He'd beat out the perennial champ, YiYi, by twelve. It was the first and last time YiYi lost. They eventually figured out that Tyler couldn't have read all four currently released Harry Potter books in one six-weeks and busted me for selling him the answers. But not before we'd already used the prize movie tickets and complimentary popcorn bucket.

He attended the local community college for two weeks before joining the volunteer firefighters and renting a house in the middle of the tennis court trucking magnate's cornfield. I would visit him when I came home from college and even felt obliged to introduce him to my wife one weekend. He walked out with an AK-47 and a new pit bull with a white coat—its blank red eyes stared us down, and I thought, well, she's from Shreveport, so maybe she's seen something like this before. She was quiet on the ride home as I tried to explain why it was a good idea to buy silver from him—*What Tyler does just has a way of working out, honey.*

Once on a visit home from college, we took my dad's Hummer around town. My dad always had two Hummers at our house—one to drive and one to maintain until the driving Hummer crapped out. So, he was the first person I called when LeBron James debuted a new Hummer during the 2022 Super Bowl.

I let Tyler drive, and, with an ice chest full of beer, we got pulled over two miles down the road. I was nervous. Not only had I come home with a 1.8 my first semester, but add a MIP to the list, and I might as well sign up for the volunteer fire department too. The officer was round and slow and had the shaved head of a policeman that looked more serious than I'd like.

He stared at us for a second before asking what was in the ice chest. I didn't know what to say. I'd go to law school after college, but even now, I still don't know the correct answer.

Tyler looked at me, shrugged, and turned back to the officer. "What do you want it to be?"

The officer laughed, and I remember him switching his radio off. "Oh, I don't know. To tell you the truth, I wouldn't mind if it were a cold beer."

"Well," said Tyler, "that's exactly what's in there, God dammit. I don't know how cold they are though, shit." He had a way of using cuss words and slang like it was punctuation.

I slumped in the heated leather seat—the Hummer's interior was built for combat and comfort, but not my growing despair.

"Shee-it!" the cop said, "Lemme take a look at what y'all got then."

Tyler hopped down, clumsily bouncing off the running boards before shuffling to the back, grabbing his jeans, and adjusting a shiny gold belt buckle as big as a bike hubcap. I froze in time as he opened the hatch, and I could hear the waving rattle of ice shifting in the chest. "See," he said, "just some beer."

The cop started shining his light around the back and into the rear-view mirror. Our eyes met for a second, and he asked Tyler to shut the trunk. I glanced back a few times. Tyler would be smoking a cigarette some of the time, laughing others. Before long, they were both back at the driver's side door - the cop studying a small piece of paper.

"Casey," the cop said, not looking up, "Casey, right?"

I nodded.

"Casey, this is your dad's car. Correct?"

"Oh, yeah… Yes, sir."

He was still studying the small white note. "Alright, well, y'all have a good night. Slow down, ya know? And I'll be seein' you, Tyler."

Tyler shut the door and shifted it down to drive. A cigarette still dangling on one lip, he rolled the window down and started to laugh, shooting me a smile out of his right eye. "You were nervous, boy!" he yelped.

"Of course, I was," I said. "What were y'all talking about?"

"Oh, he pulled me over on Ryan's go-kart two weeks ago on Kings Highway, so he knows me. And it sounds like they need a new copier at their office or something. I don't know. I gave him my card."

"You have a card? What the hell are you going to do about a copier?"

"I'm going to sell him one! I'll find one. And, of course, I have a card. You don't?"

"No. I'm in college," I said.

"What's the holdup?" Tyler said.

ꝏ

I don't talk to Tyler much these days, not from fear of being pulled back into *something*—there's nothing to be pulled back into, which I mean in the most innocuous way possible. Texarkana is not the setting of an early 90s movie about getting out and making something of yourself. A man from Texarkana ran for president, dammit (as an independent, but still)! Ragtime music was popularized by another man from Texarkana. Hell—the Texas Chainsaw Massacre was loosely based on a series of murders in the town. It's not some down-on-its-luck succubus holding hostage any inkling of talent. It's far from the Jeffrey Dahmer of cities—kidnapping and eating their own alive—instead many have left to notable lives. There are a few porn stars under our high school's Wikipedia's "Notable Alumni" section. There's a Chic-Fil-A. There's a burger place that was on *Oprah*. This reminds me—my mom was on *Oprah*. We picked up the camera crew from the Ross Perot Airport, took them by TLC (the burger place from the show), and showed them how well our dogs could sit and fetch.

Oprah's people were very impressed, but they should've gone to the Road Runner gas station off the highway, where the best burgers get made.

No, I don't call Tyler because I'd be sucked back into anything Texarkana-related. I just know nothing's changed—or at least I hope it hasn't.

Tyler met me at my house when I came in for Christmas a couple of years after college. My mom was happy to see him, and they talked about a going away party they had planned for a friend going to the Air Force. Tyler was part of a few going away parties.

Sitting around our kitchen table, he held my parents and brother in a story–I haven't seen my dad that captivated by a non-WWII documentary in my entire life.

"You know," he said without warning, "I helped catch Trace a couple of months back."

Trace? I went through our graduating class. We'd been through kindergarten through the senior year together, so I would know a Trace. "Trace McMichael," he said, probably sensing my confusion. My mom gasped, and my dad stopped shoveling ice into his milk glass.

Trace McMichael was on our little league baseball team, but he went to a different high school, so he might as well have been in another country for me.

I asked why Trace required catching. He'd shot and killed a police officer with her own gun while she was transporting him to his cell, then stolen her keys and run off in the prisoner transport van.

"Oh," I said.

Alone in the cornfield house, Tyler had his state-issued police scanner on full blast (he was now an officer of some kind in the volunteer fire department and claimed this was a necessary gadget). Soon after hearing the radio announcement, he remembered Trace's grandmother lived up the road and behind a grove of pine trees.

At this point in the story, Tyler reached into his pocket and pulled out his cell phone.

"They let me record the entire police interview."

"You have a recorded police interview on your phone?" I said.

"I do. Is that okay?"

I was in my second year of law school. I had no idea if that's okay.

"So, yeah. They called me in, and, well, and I'll just play it for y'all. The audio is okay, I guess."

The four of us hovered above an early-model iPhone on my mom's tiled kitchen countertops. The tiles had little crawfish, pelicans, or shrimp painted every fourth or fifth one and reflected the buzzing lights of the kitchen right into your eye each morning.

Muffled voices scratched through the speakers when he hit play.

"*Okay, okay*," Tyler's voice said, "I'm *going to record, so this is on the up and up*." I immediately began to laugh at the show. It was very much like Tyler to be so openly honest and hostile.

"*So, you turn on your scanner and hear what?*"

"That's one of the guys interviewing me," Tyler told us before my dad waved him off.

"*I hear Trace McMichael is on the run and just killed some lady!*" There was a long pause before I heard Tyler exhaling. "*Can I smoke in here? So, then I knew he would be coming to see his grandmother because she basically raised him, and I know he doesn›t have enough sense not to come to the exact place where everyone knows he›s going, and I know he doesn›t usually take the right way. He goes behind my house and up by the creek, but what he should do is go in front of my house. The way he usually goes is dangerous as hell.»*

"*Why is it dangerous?*" someone in the room asks.

"*Because there's no lights, and there's a creek. And,*" he paused again, another exhale, "*I figured he'd be in some kind of hurry. So, I grabbed my gun—you guys have been to my house, and I think I showed you my guns, and they're all registered—so, I grab my AK, load it, then I called y'all and said he was probably headed this way.*"

"*And why the AK?*"

"*Because it shoots fast, and it's loud, I'd just traded my other machine gun for that school bus out front, and I didn't know what Trace had.*"

Around this time, I looked over to see my mom, mouth open, both hands gripping Tyler's. Clutching them up by her chin like he was in peril, staring at the phone in disbelief.

"*Enough with the interruptions,*" Tyler's voice sounded irritated. "*Like I said, I grabbed my AK, and I have an extensive security system around the house. And I have Bo.*" Bo was the white pitbull. Bodacious, Bo for short, named after a BBQ place in town. Bo attacked my dog, a white Labrador retriever I named Paul Revere after a Beastie Boys song, a couple of months before this incident, so my ears perked up at Bo's mention, but I was also transfixed on Tyler's voice. He was confident in the tape like he knew he'd be playing it to parents and friends around an oddly painted kitchen counter. And what did he have to be so confident about—me, a second-year law student with an apartment in the big city and a girlfriend from another *sorta* big city, had been shouted down by a campus security guard a week before for parking on the stripe—so where did *he* get this from?

"*So, I've got cameras everywhere. Everywhere. I turned on the floodlights and hunkered down behind the front door. It wasn't long before here he comes, and, my house, y'all have been to my house, but my house is—what's the right word – it's on blocks. That makes it sound shitty, but it isn't. It's a nice house, but it's on blocks.*"

"Pier and beam, Tyler," my dad says, laughing a sort of high-pitched giggle that he usually reserves for the comedic icebreaker in a western.

"*Since it's on blocks, you can hear someone walking inside from outside the house. So, like, if I ran to the back of the house, he'd hear me if he was close enough. So, I decided to use the intercom system. I yelled at him, I yelled through it, 'Trace! Get up to the front, man!' and he curled around my yard, the mowed part, around the bus and that tractor they keep out there, then he starts looking in my truck, so I said hell Nah and went outside on the front porch.*"

I felt my brother pacing around the kitchen counter, both hands on his head like he'd run wind sprints.

"*I went out, kept Bo inside because he's really a big baby, and I said, 'Trace—man—I know what happened, and you need to get outta here and get away from me and my truck. I'm serious, man.' And I'm holding the gun up now, and he can see me, and he says, 'Are you going to shoot me, Tyler?' in that kinda slow mumble that he's got, and I said, 'Go to your grandma's, and I'll leave it alone. I did call the cops, though, so there's that.' And then he starts crying. He was crying for a second, then he asked me what he was gonna do. He said, 'I didn't mean to,' and he takes a step towards me, and I dunno. I just shot. I aimed at his feet, but I don't know how many times y'all've heard an AK-47, a real AK-47, not that Academy Sports shit, a real AK-47. Well, I shot it at his feet, and he was out of there. I could see him running through the corn, falling a few times, but I knew he'd go and try to steal his grandma's car or something like that. Sure enough, the cops, maybe one of you, got there right after and caught him.*"

Tyler reached out and tapped his phone screen. The raspy whine of the recording stopped, and he looked around, a knowing grin across his face.

"Tyler," my mom said, shaking her head with what looked like exhaustion, "Tyler, I don't know what to say."

I must've made him play it for me ten times that night. I couldn't get over the smoking. He was in a police interview, talking about his house on blocks and shooting at a future death row inmate, all with the bravado of Wyatt Earp.

ග

Three years after the kitchen conversation, around 2014, he invited me to the country club to play golf before his stepbrother Ryan, the one with the go-kart, left for college on a full golf scholarship.

The summer before this, Ryan had been invited to the Under-18 World Invitational Tournament in South Africa. He spent most of his time at Tyler's cornfield house smoking pot but was one of thirty kids in the world invited to this event. We didn't watch the tournament, but we watched the televised welcome dinner, where they filmed each kid as they announced their entrance to the dining hall. The dining room on the TV was bright and had golden rods hanging white curtains and drapes about the room. The camera, positioned at the front of the room, tracked each contestant down a narrow hallway after their name was called. We'd see an awkward but usually tall, thin kid bumble around the corner, up the green carpeted hallway, and enter the dining room to applause. Tyler narrated each catwalk. "This is the kid that won the tournament. He sat at Ryan's table."

"Casey, man, you notice what every kid is wearing?" Tyler said, pointing to a short blond boy skipping down the hallway. "Each one of 'em."

"A tux? A cummerbund?"

"Man," Tyler said, teetering on the edge of a brown, roach colored couch—its slipcover salted with Bo's hair—with one of those smiles so big it starts in your eyes. "Ryan doesn't have a tux. Or if he does, he didn't pack it. Ho-lee chit! You're at a nice dinner, I told him, there's people there from Antarctica probably, I warned him. You flew thousands of miles to be there, et cetera, et cetera..." He said this last part miming a symphony conduction—then fell back into the couch still smiling—an exuberant, exhausted Bernstein from Bowie County. "You might want to dress up a little bit, right? Wait 'til you see old boy here in a second."

A few moments later, Ryan's name was called, and in almost the perfect sequence, he came from around a different corner than the rest, and he was in a polo shirt, khaki pants, and flip-flops. And he didn't stop in the clearly formed line at the end of the hallway, instead strolling around and taking his seat off camera. All the social cues in the world, but he couldn't be bothered.

Tyler was howling and rewinding to the moment Ryan came into view. He spent the rest of the night cussing Bo for jumping on the couch, wrestling him to the ground, both biting the other's ear.

Back on the course in 2014, we tinkered around the greens, kicking our ball up hills and betting on who could keep it on the fairway. With his cigarette and NASCAR golf bag, Tyler showed me how far a 158-pound man could hit a 1.62-ounce ball, and we talked about what was next—a trip out of the country, degrees, and women.

I realized we only talked about me.

My family were country club members, and I'd spent most summers there splashing around the pool, ordering extra cheese on my burgers—it was a big summer when they got the Choco-Taco in back. Still, Tyler paraded me around the course like it was my first time, showing me nooks and crannies I didn't know existed, like a pine needle-covered hole off the fourteenth green where he hid the weed he'd sell to the doctors and lawyers on the course. I'd graduated from law school and definitely knew this was probably not allowed under state or federal law—one of them, surely. The image of Tyler's golf bag, its checkerboard font scrolled down the sides, mixed with the Callaway, Srixon, and Nike bags outside the drenched concrete kart wash, didn't seem out of place. Tiger Woods had played here, and there was a picture of him in the clubhouse to prove it, but the highlighter yellow racing caution flag on the ball carrier side of his bag, that Tyler used for beer, fit. And I still don't know why.

"Man, Casey," he'd said that day, telling me about being a dad to his new twin sons. "I want to be a better guy than I have been, I guess. God dammit, I don't know what I need to do or what book I need to read to be a good fuckin' person—be Catholic, Methodist, Jehovah's Witness. Hell, I'll read the Quran if I have to. Just want to be a good guy and raise my kids right." He paused, "Je-he-sus Cry-st it's hard. You'll see.

"Life, man, life sometimes is like figuring out the problem with a Nissan—you had one, so you know what I'm sayin." I nodded but didn't understand. "You gotta take the wheels off, take out the bottom and shit, just to get inside and die-ag-knows the issue. But once you get to it, it's just like every other car. I've got a good thing going here but I don't look down on anybody else."

Tyler did have a good thing going—living only a few miles from where we'd grown up, ridden bikes, knocked over mailboxes, had our first beer, where Jeffrey Keenan—a Boeing engineer—had consumed a five-foot piece of beef jerky, and from where Tyler had fought our local movie buff after a game of wall-ball went wrong until Mr. Wayne broke it up on his blue tractor—Mr. Wayne worked in maintenance at the high school but drove his tractor all over town. His shrill, twang voice carried as much weight as the tractor (he got them to stop by asking them if they were "fixin' to fight or fuck?"). Tyler sees my parents more than I do, always reminding them of the hours he and I spent trapped in our laundry chute as kids. He was happy and home. Like a cat scared of its shadow, it can run and leap and hiss all it wants, sometimes finding reprieve in the shade, but it'll always be there in the light. Like Texarkana was for me.

ꕥ

I always thought east Texas, or at least Texarkana, lacked any real definable characteristic. Most regions have a food staple or culture that stands out on the map somewhere—we had the highest-grossing Applebee's two years in a row.

There's a spot at the post office where you can stand in two places at once, but I recently found out that you can do that at the Hoover Dam, and there's some monument in Arizona where you can stand in four states at once. What else was left for us without this novelty on the sediment outskirts of the Dallas suburbs? We'd always have Oprah, I assumed.

But when I look back, I think about the definable characteristics of the people that make that area. Many of us crawling, fighting, biting, clawing to get out of it and run—falling over one another to make it to Dallas, Houston,

Austin, or Little Rock, and to leave something we or I never really understood, like fire ants racing over a bare foot straddled in the pine needles. Others biting down hard, clamping onto the fleshy way of life, scrambling back down the interstates to get home, not retreating from success or failure but the satisfying feeling of things that will always be there and people that don't need to change. Flip flops at a dinner in South Africa and my friend Tyler.

Someone asked me what my relationship with Tyler was like now—and there isn't one, I told her. Or, at least, it's been a while. I see him at Clay's memorial golf tournament when I'm able to make it, knowing full well he'll be front row for the Beach Boys cover band they rent each year. We went to get dinner after the tournament last year, and Tyler insisted he had a coupon at Pizza Inn, a dimly lit chain buffet connected to an indoor swimming pool so the whole place smelled like chlorine. We ate our fill of peperoni and chocolate pizzas before he politely offered to get the check, brandishing the coupon from his pocket—a small, jagged piece of metal. Without breaking the story of how this girl we grew up had recently found God, Tyler stuck the little razor in his mouth and sliced his gums right above his front teeth, and called our waiter over to demand our meal be comped on account of his blood soaked grin. The manager, sweating and stammering, didn't know how that could've gotten into the pizza dough, but he was certain Tyler would never have to pay for another meal at that particular franchise location.

If I saw Tyler tomorrow, he'd remind me I owe him a pizza buffet, and he'd know me better than anyone in the room. Does he know about my inner desires or my recent bout with hemorrhoids as well as my wife? Probably not, but are the hemorrhoids the real me? I hope not.

I don't resent Tyler for tolerating such a simple life, but I do love him for it sometimes. I miss him and my hometown, which occupy the same space in my brain. Ambition doesn't always run uphill, and Tyler's full of whatever people have that make them stay in a place like East Texas and what make the roots so hard to dig through.

ꝏ

Tyler passed away in March of 2025. This essay came out before he died, and Tyler called me with a few changes he'd like to see—which I greatly appreciated and promptly made. I told him that, through a connection in Los Angeles, and mostly by chance, I'd met Larry David who had read this essay and wanted to know if Tyler was real and if he could meet him. I laughed it away with Mr. David—attempting to seem aloof and out-of-the-way, which is my default mode around famous people—but I was excited to tell Tyler.

He let me finish the whole story before asking, politely, "Dude—who *the fuck* is Larry David?"

Tyler's funeral was what you would hope. I came to the visitation the day before, stood in line to see his sister Taryn, and right before I got there a girl in one of those thick, early-2000s looking belts—like a fashionable leather weight belt—said something to Taryn that caused the funeral director escorted the girl out. "Hey, Casey," Taryn said, with an arm around my neck. I asked what just happened. "Oh, nothing. Just aboutta have to beat some ass."

His pallbearers wore fishing shirts and nice belt buckles at the funeral, and I watched a woman pack multiple Zyn pouches deep into the cervices of her lip. A preacher screamed at the audience to stop crying and rejoice because we didn't know better than Jesus, and Jesus needed Tyler more than we did. It was the middle of the Lent, and my Lenten offering that year was to not let people influence my thoughts on God or religion (keep in mind Trump's Senior Advisor to the White House Faith Office was offering salvation and to turn God into a weapon of mass destruction against your enemies for a simple offering of one thousand dollars). I failed that day.

In our last conversation, a few months before his passing, Tyler told me about getting airlifted after cutting his hand open while working with a saw. According to Tyler, he tied a tourniquet with the belt from his Budweiser work uniform, drank a bottle of Jack Daniels, and waited for the ambulance peacefully on the porch. He got on the helicopter, heckled the pilot about his age and made sure he'd heard of Kobe Bryant, then passed out and woke up in the OR "without my hat, so I freaked out tryna find my hat." I asked what kind of hat it was, excited for a small, unique detail I might use later. "Oh, I don't remember," he said. "I just like hats—not everything means something."

Maybe it doesn't. When I heard he'd passed away, I was writing at a coffee shop in Baton Rouge. I stood up, packed my things, and walked back to my car. I had my writing playlist in my headphones—mostly lyric-less jazz I've modeled entirely off the *Hey Arnold!* soundtrack—and a piano came on. I liked it. It reminded me of Tyler. When I got to my car and turned it on, the song came up—*Solace* by Scott Joplin. Another Texarkana legend like Tyler Ashley.

Modern Baptists

"I know that guy," I said. "I know him."

"No, you don't," Stuart laughed, looking at me like I was a Mardi Gras float come to life. "There's no way."

ര

I always associate New Orleans tourists with New Jersey because I once sublet a room in a four-bedroom house during a clerkship in my law school years, and all four of my roommates were from New Jersey. Talon was a budding stunt double in town for the nascent film industry. Chandler was in construction and quickly brought to anger when I refused to pay my part of the utility bill because, as I explained over a bowl of cereal one morning while he stood hunched over me with a wrench, I showered at the courthouse, so my utility usage was minimal. Juliet was a Tulane student that I'm still Facebook friends with, from south New Jersey, as she would say, which meant nothing to me. Johnny was Juliet's boyfriend and stayed over most nights. According to her latest update, Juliet got engaged and married—not to Johnny. Good job, Juliet.

Before law school and the uncomfortable breakfast inquisition, I was in uptown New Orleans during Mardi Gras season sometime around 2009. I was a sophomore in college and experiencing what true hedonism looked like underneath a yellow visor someone told me looked good. All apartments in New Orleans are damp, and because they're damp, they smell—it is one of the many quirks that passersby, again probably from New Jersey, seem to love. My friend Stuart brought me a cup of coffee from a hand grinder—the first I'd ever seen. I would soon see my next on a painstaking road trip with my brother from San Antonio to Portland, Oregon where he did his medical residency. He refused to let me stop at even a gas station for what he deemed "corporate coffee." Instead, I drank mushy, grainy bean water out of the trunk of his car each morning. It was always never hot but always warm enough to make me think I was drinking a loogie.

Stuart's coffee was hot, but the refrigerator didn't work, so milk wasn't an option. We reviewed last night's events. I'd seen Mardi Gras before but never from the underbelly. The costumes, the drugs, the girls, the guys, the black people, the white people, and the passing celebrity—always white—on a balcony or building step, just taking it all in like he was some overseer of a tremendous human feast.

I sipped the coffee and arched my back. The coils of the apartment's couch dug into my neck and legs, somehow simultaneously, throughout much of the night, and I was worried the red gash around the back of my head might be mistaken for an overly aggressive hickey or worse—might not be. "No," I'd say, "just an old wire I slept with last night."

Some form of vodka oozed out of my tongue each time I shut my mouth, which served as an unpleasant reminder of events but also made the coffee more bearable. I've long been an unadmirer of coffee, particularly in its natural state. I'd rather a glass of milk with a single bean dropped in as a surprise caffeinated choking hazard.

I thought about the coffee, Stuart's roommate named, simply, Beach, and how hot I was, when I heard a familiar voice.

"Repent!" it said, with a slight East Texas drawl. "Repent," it whispered this time.

ꕥ

I half assumed I was the only one that could hear it. Stuart grew up in Lafayette, in Louisiana's midsection, which is as much a Catholic stronghold as it is a city named after a French aristocrat, so he wouldn't have any pent-up memories of protestant preachers and their ne'er-do-well youth ministers traipsing around the public school system with free McDonald's for anyone that would sit and "chat"—which was always such a loaded word.

I was once *Signed Up 4 Saving* my eighth-grade year in return for a free double quarter pounder with cheese. "Get saved in four days at the FBC. Your friends will be there, your parents will be there, Jesus will be there, and we'll have pancakes and burgers—are you saved, Casey?" I didn't know how he knew my name. What a rush. He had jet black hair that he gelled into a single spike shooting up from the top of his head. His name was Kevin, but he went by Kev, and everybody knew him. I signed up and faced my mother's wrath at home.

I whined, "But they said they'd have a band, and it's on Wednesday night, and I'll be saved by Saturday. St. Edwards," our small Catholic church across town, "St. Edwards takes six months!" My mom shook her head and went down the syllabus of other catholic kids in town to see if they took the processed meat bait. Adam was from Illinois, the Chicago area, and his family had been in town for twelve years, and his mom still didn't let him sleep over anywhere on Saturday nights so he wouldn't miss Mass. Tommy was from Argentina but flirted with some of the girls at First Baptist Church, FBC, so he went from time to time but mainly to play basketball. Johnathan liked McDonald's too much to pass it up at the time—he's since lost over one hundred pounds and was featured with Terry Bradshaw in a Nutrisystem commercial. Peter—that's who my mom was most interested in—Peter's mom was from Ireland, and they made a pilgrimage once a year. Somewhere. Not to Ireland, specifically, but to some Catholic monument.

"Of course, Peter didn't sign up," she said over the phone. I looked down, fear in my throat. "I'll call the school tomorrow," she said. And she would, but the school wouldn't do anything about it. Yes, she told me, I have been saved, and I should tell people that—Kev especially. Protesting was little use—this was a woman resigned to take our only annual family picture for the church directory. All of us gussied up in our hand-me-down dresses and slacks sitting against the blue backdrop in the small laminated book our church put out every year, then we'd use as a Christmas card months later.

ꝏ

"Repentance is a cornerstone of a life with Jesus Christ," the soft, deep-fried voice continued.

ꝏ

Something about someone saying Jesus Christ always makes my right eye twitch. Not in any old way, but an East Texas twang will get a solid eye closure. "Je-he-zus Cry-st" is the closest etymological spelling. Catholics talk about God or Mary mostly, but Baptists, from my experience, really honed in on Jesus—his whereabouts, his doings, his musing, and his dialogue. His dialogue was of most significance. Every year of elementary and middle school, 90% of my school would participate in something called "Bible Drill." They'd all run around with slips of paper stuffed into their pockets or overflowing from their backpacks, each with a different bible verse scribbled on the back and the name on the front.

Walking the halls that week, you'd bear witnesses to an ancient duel of fates between red-faced kids leaning on lockers, their pockets filled with scriptures and Accutane prescriptions. The drill would start with one announcing, "Draw weapons!" enthusiastically followed by the other pulling out a bible or a stack of white paper strips. "Joshua 1:9!"

Then a few steps down, "Romans 8:28!" followed closely by a "Shit! I knew you'd say that!"

"Psalm 34:4-5, 8!"

"Oh, dammit—Umm—come on—umm—*I sought the Lord, and He answered me and delivered me from all my fears*," followed by a deep breath, "*Those who look to Him are radiant, and their faces shall never be ashamed. Oh, taste and see that the LORD is good! Blessed is the man who takes refuge in Him*! Ha—boom!"

The school let all the Baptist kids leave on the Thursday of Bible Drill to ride a bus to Little Rock or Dallas, or Waco—probably Waco—for the competition. One year I had to watch as Kristen, a Methodist and the object of my affection, boarded the rocking bus, chanting Jesus's name. I once went to the Methodist youth group and won a pancake eating contest. When I came home and told my mom, she was disappointed in more ways than one.

No Bible Drill for me and Peter and Tommy. Adam got to go because his mom let him try new and exciting things like this. The teachers put on a movie—Pearl Harbor one year—for the stragglers on Thursday and Friday—the Catholic kids and most likely the black kids whose parents once asked the school to prioritize a secular education and five days a week.

ꕤ

"Repent—NOW!"

I shook my head in New Orleans and looked around the room. Stuart was grinning from ear to ear, staring blankly at the T.V. "Look at this guy," he said, his hand searching for something on the coffee table, jumping around to different spots until it landed in a water cup. "There must me like ten thousand people there."

I craned my neck and saw a familiar grayish-blue carpet and almost movie theater backdrop. It was the First Baptist Church in Texarkana, Texas—on T.V. in New Orleans on a Sunday. Pastor Joe, as he called himself, strutted across an extended platform while the camera slowly panned to a group of well-dressed men nodded violently with each word, their coats and pastel ties shaking with anticipation for the Lord.

"I know that guy," I said. "I *know* him."

"No, you don't," Stuart laughed. "There's no way."

"I do," I said, sitting up and bracing for a spring to catch me in the wrong area, "And that's where – that church is where we graduated from high school. It's the biggest building in town. Bigger than the football stadium, I think."

"No way. Is he always yelling like this?" My focus shifted back to Pastor Joe. His light brown suit and tan turtleneck fit snug around his shoulders, and his bald head shown in the camera lights. He wasn't always yelling. In fact, I'd never heard him raise his voice before this morning, when my headache really needed him to stop.

"He never yelled," I said. "I've never been to church there, though, so maybe he does on Sundays? Why is this on T.V. down here? Why are we watching it—and so loud?"

"I don't know man, I just thought it was interesting. I've never seen anything like this before."

This reminded me of my AP (Advanced Placement but someone asked in our Pre-AP classes sophomore year if it stood for "Axcellence Program"—they didn't make it into the next round of schooling) European History class my junior year of high school. Flipping around the pages of atrocities in our antiquated books, the soon-to-be Salutatorian for the class ahead of mine raised his hand near the end of the second semester to genuinely inquire: "Mrs. Suddeth, are there any more around today? Are they still here?" Are what still here, she asked. "Catholics? Do they still exist?" he said again.

She had to think about it.

I myself questioned it a few times, and now here was Stuart watching the show—staring at Pastor Joe like a lab rat in a maze. A friend of mine, I suspect a red-headed kid named Kyle, put me on the prayer list at FBC my senior year of high school, and Pastor Joe called my house every day for two weeks. Each time he left a voicemail explaining that someone cared about Casey—*Jeez-zus Cry-st* cared. I thought it was pretty funny until my mom answered one day.

"The Bible?" she said, "Of course we read the Bible in our house!" She started scrambling around the kitchen counter, careful not to twist the phone's spiral cord. She opened a few drawers, the mail slot, and finally, the cookbook cabinet. "I always have one handy in case Casey wants to sit down and read." She turned to me and shrugged. "Go find a bible somewhere," she said through her teeth, her hand over the bottom of the phone.

When I came back, she was off the phone and laughing. "That just burns me up," she said, shutting a cabinet hard enough that I took an involuntary step back. "I'll tell you when to read the bible—not him."

ꝏ

"Turn this off, man," I said. Stuart was transfixed on the movement, the theater of it all. Stuart was a product of south Louisiana Catholic daycare, Catholic elementary, middle, and high school, as are most of the people I know down here. When my sister graduated from the University of Texas in Austin, the keynote speaker told the crowd about Texas culture and how it would only grow and bloom in the hands of the right caretakers—my friends in Louisiana laughed about this and asked what Texas culture really was besides cows and boots. I didn't have an answer, but looking at the pastor move and shake the crowd and walls, I thought it a bit embarrassing but this was the passion I'd grown to know. The most Stuart had seen a priest move was an elbow or two, and here was a genuine acrobat working the static electricity up across the carpeted stage. I saw someone play a trumpet at a Methodist church in Texarkana once after the rare occasion my mom let me sleep over at a non-Catholic friend's house on a Saturday night, so I knew what Stuart was going through—that first bout of genuine amusement and confusion colliding into an exciting communion. I'd again have the same feeling years later when my friend Worm and I drove through Provo, Utah. Worm—not from south Louisiana but north, near the same overworn holes of the Bible Belt as myself—was whatever religion didn't believe in dinosaurs. He laughed hysterically on the road trip when, passing through Denver, my sister took us to see some petrified dinosaur tracks on a white ridge outside of town. But in Provo, on a Sunday in the summer, the town was ripe for tumbleweeds until we turned a corner near BYU's campus and laid eyes on at least two thousand modestly dressed, mostly denim skirts and white shirts, Mormons our age—all seemingly married or at least pushing baby strollers. We zipped along a quarter mile quietly in the Prius we'd borrowed from his dad, surrounded by smiles and an onslaught of people striding into the street to stop our car with an outstretched wave. Worm, either from genuine fright or the effects of a weed brownie we'd eaten that morning, cracked the window each time, barely enough to get his nose out of it, and said, "Uhhh… we just want food and to get out of here. No trouble."

They all laughed before confirming nothing, "Not even the ethnic stuff," as they said, was open on Sundays in Provo. We continued like this to Salt Lake, where Worm refused to enter the Tabernacle and asked a man in an Alabama football shirt if everything was on the up and up around town—the man turned with a long smile and an even longer line of children running up to greet the North Louisiana native who could only muster a short "Fuck Alabama!" before sprinting away, angry with me and the rest of the cabal of dinosaur conspirators.

Back in New Orleans, Stuart kept flipping around the channels until he found a show that was just coming out about five Italians on the Jersey coast—probably all Catholic.

I was secretly proud of Texarkana. The big time, I thought. On T.V. as far south as New Orleans and a pretty clear picture, too. Now that I've lived in Louisiana for fifteen years, just about as long as I was sentient in Texas, I'm even more convinced FBC is a necessary addition to the landscape of coddled Catholics around me now with their easy access to masses, education, and religious amenities—they have a fair at the Catholic churches down here just to attract new members, and my daughter loves the Ferris wheel at all of them. Even the public schools have fish on Fridays during Lent in South Louisiana—Texarkana had Steak Finger Fridays during the Lenten season, meaning I had a pre-packed PB&J. FBC and their ilk spice up the standard order of things in a world like religion that can stale faster than a communion wafer.

Besides, it was always the non-denominational kids you had to really look out for.

A man in New Orleans held up a JESUS SAVES poster while balancing a megaphone in his other hand. The poster was neon yellow and stapled to a pair of fence posts he'd rigged into a cross. He'd scream for everyone to repent. Or that the apocalypse was nigh. He'd mentioned hell and Satan's influence on the town. It's not Satan, my man. It's the unscrupulous temptation of the tourism industry.

Every now and then, someone that had too much, probably from

New Jersey, stepped to the megaphone and screamed back at the man. And always, like a stolen valor video on YouTube, it's the one that confronts him that makes it hard to watch. He'd lower his megaphone and shout bible verses inches from the tourist's ear. He must have been an absolute menace at Bible Drill, I thought. They usually had a young kid, moderately dressed, flanking their hip. A look of determined acceptance in the kids' eyes, like they were almost convinced everyone on the street was doomed but themselves, but they also liked video games or another vice.

The Texarkana Baptists lacked this type of violent panache, more like a vanilla bean or a glass of milk—they possessed a dullness. I went to a sleepaway baseball camp for a few years but didn't find out it was Christian until a decade later when my mom transferred all our VHS tapes to DVD. She asked if I wanted to see the tapes from camp, and we sat down to see the opening prayer. And the 7th-inning stretch and Gospel. And then the closing conversations. What was this, I asked. "Oh, they tried to convert everyone. You don't remember me having a talk with your cabin's counselor about staying away from you with that stuff—his chewing tobacco and the Bible?"

I didn't. All I knew is I wasn't allowed to go to the regular sleepaway camp because everyone came back with promise rings and chastity belts—woven themselves in the weaving class.

My family, apart from being one of the few Catholic ones in town, also stood out for our diets—I can count on one hand the times my mom served up barbeque or steak for dinner, Texas staples. We were a seafood and bread family. More etouffees than Frito chili pies. More shrimp boils than briskets. We weren't Texas people in many ways, but that didn't make us not Texarkana.

This would be my last Mardi Gras as an aimless college student. That night, back and forth over the boundary between unacceptable harassment and passionate protestation, the man with the JESUS SAVES sign bumped me, and I twisted my ankle. Then somewhere on a steamy, stinking street corner, I believe someone snuck a grenade into my beer, and I woke up the next day in a stranger's house. There was a chorus of at least eight dogs, different shapes, colors, and barking volumes. They followed me around the old house, their feet scratched and tapped across the creaking wooden floors, only stopping to roll on any rug we found with me limping along. I tried opening the front and back doors, both locked from the outside. I found a study with a bookcase leaned against what I assumed were windows, a small line of light stretched between the shelves across the floor. Picture frames crammed into every corner of the room's wooden walls, some stuffed into bookcase shelves, and others stacked on a dark brown desk. I scanned a row of pictures, noticing each had two people standing side-by-side, smiling at the camera. It was the type of thing someone might use Instagram for now—some throwaway pictures of you with friends or something I expect to see in a kitschy Italian restaurant—but the man in each image looked familiar. My 2009 flip phone didn't have the internet, so I couldn't look him up, but I knew him from somewhere. It hit me—on my roommate's wall in the freshman year dorm was a poster from *The Graduate*. These were all pictures of Dustin Hoffman, but for some reason—maybe the printer toner was low—it didn't like look Dustin Hoffman's pictures. Some were professional photographs, while others appeared scanned from a Xerox. Others a picture of a picture. Some were with the Pope, but the Pope didn't look natural on the red carpet for whatever movie premier Dustin Hoffman attended. I did a slow heel turn on a green rug, half expecting to find a young Hoffman with a baggy brown corduroy blazer over an untucked blue button-down, kind of shrugging his shoulders.

I went to the kitchen, loudly yelped a few times to see if anyone would respond with some human noise, then broke a small window above the sink and climbed out. I landed in bushes off Prytanea Street, only three houses from Stuart's apartment. My car was nestled between garbage bins two blocks past that. I contemplated the possibility I'd had some kind of *experience* with Dustin Hoffman as I galloped to my car, limping with my sore ankle. Once there, I bid adieu to my toothbrush and phone charger in Stuart's apartment, texted the group I'd driven down two days before that I was leaving and they should find another ride and scooted out of New Orleans with my engine roaring up the oak covered streets to the comfort of the hardscrabble interstate.

If the good Pastor could see me now, I thought.

Since writing this essay, I was regretful to learn the good pastor had since transformed into a Facebook wielding political pundit.

Mud Bugs

Sometimes things just happen without your express knowledge when you're younger—like a birthday party being planned, or a trip to the grocery store, or a divorce. That's how I, on a spring day in fourth grade, found out WCW Monday Night Nitro was coming to the ArkLaTex, and I'd be going.

WCW, the acronym for World Championship Wrestling, Inc., was the closest I had to an addiction before hitting puberty. Every Monday night I was hanging around our big screen in the cramped living room, drifting from a big blue cloth ottoman to the couch, pacing in a line near the fireplace, waiting for my mom to shake her head and flip over to TNT for what would surely be an hour of nonstop bombardment.

I shared this passion with most of the fourth grade. We all had our favorites.

There were the guys that liked Raven's Flock—Raven, a long-haired, thick-bodied wrestler that sported cutoff jean shorts past the knee, a leather jacket, and a scowl, fought dirty. His flock wouldn't burst into the ring so much as meander into it. Whatever they did, it was clear they didn't want to be there but would kick some ass anyway. They had a small band of followers at school—the grunge kids that were already into Nirvana, which wasn't as cool in the 90s as it is today, but they probably had older siblings. To claim the flock as your absolute favorite meant disappointment most Monday nights. One of the members, Kidman, had a finishing move called the shooting star press—he'd do a gainer off the top ropes, landing square on another man's chest. The move was and is still the coolest thing I've ever seen.

There was the old guard—Ric Flair, Rowdy Roddy Piper, Randy Savage, and Hulk Hogan. We later linked a friend's mom, consistently single since his birth, to her time working at a fledgling WCW in 1988 as Flair's assistant, around nine months before her son's birth. His blond hair raises questions to this day.

There were the popular ones, the top billers—Lex Luger, Scott Hall, Buff Bagwell (who my roommate in college had a signed headshot of), The Giant, Chris Jericho, and Goldberg, to name a few. All of them big, white, and greasy. They'd strut into the ring with enough bravado to alert the authorities but still an inkling of the *every man*. Like Diamond Dallas Page who looked more like a long-haul trucker or Mötley Crüe drummer than acrobat. They were a marketer's wet dream. Your dad liked these guys.

Lex Luger flexed hard enough that his bicep turned into a knot the size of a honeydew melon. It wasn't until years later I'd find out this wasn't natural, but none of it was, and it didn't matter. I cheered Barry Bonds, Mark McGuire, and Roger Clemens with gusto, and none of them could do a backflip off a wobbling tight rope.

There were the high-flyers, the lightweight guys like Rey Mysterio Jr., Juventud Guerrera, Eddie Guerrero, and Psicosis. Most of them donned elaborate luchador masks that would eventually be removed in a show of ultimate disrespect. They were the closest most of the rural south would get to Cirque Du Soleil. And, as the names would suggest, they were almost always Mexican.

I'd often wake my brother, a sophomore in high school at this time, from naps with Eddie Guerrero's signature frog splash. Jumping off his bed's banister, doing a sit up mid-air, then landing on David's mouth. I stopped for two reasons: first, Eddie Guerrero beat Juventud Guerrera in a match and removed his mask which I found distasteful, and second, my brother played dead one morning and punched me in the nose mid-air.

WCW had a way of introducing its audience to unique cultures. Mexican people were acrobats. People from Texas, like the hard-nosed Dean Malenko, wore cowboy hats and only talked about Texas. Homosexuals were really into disco, or at least Disco Inferno was acting in more ways than one. Hulk Hogan's runout music, Voodoo Child, was my first exposure to Jimi Hendrix. But, above all, people from Harlem could kick.

The Harlem Heat—a duo of brothers named Booker T and Stevie Ray—were the only iteration of Harlem in my life until a trip from the Globetrotters in ninth grade. My friend Clint was in a walking boot and crutches when they brought him out on the court to shoot a half-court shot. He made it. Needless to say, the bar was set high when I learned about Zora Neal Hurston, Langston Hughes, and Countee Cullen the next year in sophomore English.

My one black friend, Andre, would showcase the latest Booker T move at recess on Tuesdays. They had a sort of side drop kick that sent their heels into an opponent's forehead. It was hard to replicate on the playground.

Goldberg was one of the only non-pretty boys of the popular bunch. His bald head usually accompanied some dark stubble around his cheeks, and his hairy chest—too overgrown to be considered sexy—gave him a rough around the edges look that sat well with me. I'm reminded of it often when I sucker my wife into taking the clippers to my back twice a year.

Goldberg started undefeated in the WCW. His finishing move, the jackhammer, was unimportant. The showstopper was him crouching in the corner of the ring, stalking his opponent who was either dazed or hilariously celebrating what he thought was a sure win. When they finally turned around, he was already mid-sprint, spearing them through the mid-section and sending the crowd into full throttle. It was the closest thing to a walk off home run that wrestling offered—an instant explosion of joy and shock wrapped into one predictable but enchanting athletic achievement.

My parents got me a Goldberg shirt one Christmas. It had barbed wire across the front, his signature tattoo, and a snarling Goldberg with the phrase "Who's next?" in gold lettering. We came home from midnight Mass and, as custom allows, were to open one special gift before going to bed. This hors d'œuvre was usually reserved for rosaries, gifts from grandparents, or something to wear the next day. But that year I tore open a box, slipped on the black and gold Goldberg shirt, and flexed and growled for the next twenty-four hours.

I didn't take it off until we went back to school a couple of weeks later, and when I did, my mom threw it and its snot-ridden sleeves into the trash.

ଓ

Now's a good time to highlight the differences between the two major wrestling leagues of the 1990s. The WCW was a countermeasure to the WWF. The WWF was an older league and for an older crowd, by my estimation. They had Stone Cold Steve Austin to the WCW's Hulk Hogan. Stone Cold would run out and smash beers over his head, all while the crowd flailed John 3:16 signs over their heads. Stone Cold was the perfect contradiction and consummate pro. Hogan ran in with an American flag.

I wasn't allowed to watch WWF for a few reasons. There were women, there was copper, and there was Vince McMahon. My parents were ahead of the curve on him. But so were plenty of parents—there was a palpable difference in WCW and WWF kids. WWF kids could cuss at an early age. They were more than likely snowboarders, not skiers, if they'd seen snow in mountain form at all. I assume today they have a higher probability of cheating on their spouses or regularly buying lottery tickets. There was no Undertaker in WCW. We had clean shaven, strait-laced guys like Chris Benoit.

ꟹ

That spring when my friend Cale, a Macho Man Randy Savage fan, told me his dad got tickets to a Monday Night Nitro, I went blank. *The* Monday Night Nitro? Looking back, no. It was a filler show to make some money on a Wednesday or Thursday as the troop of traveling fighters went from Dallas to New Orleans or Memphis.

The next day my mom told me, a reluctant look in her eye, that I'd be going too. I was confused. Sure, they got me pay-per-view for Halloween Havoc the year before, and they would again for Bash at the Beach that spring, but these were small potatoes compared to a real event.

"Are you even excited?" my mom asked.

"Yes…" I said, collecting myself.

"Who do you want to see? The one with the face paint?"

She was talking about Sting. And yes, that is who I wanted to see. He was the Timberlake to the rest of the league's N*SYNC. He had jet black hair that he wore long and sometimes in his painted white face, thin black trail lines from his eyes and mouth looked like an emo tiger. Think Brandon Lee from The Crow, but in a black trench coat with a baseball bat. Depending on the curves of the black lines, it might look like he was the devil or sort of sad when he, unlike the other guys, repelled from the rafters on a cord or simply appeared after a momentary blackout. In this way he was never in a hurry. People always look flustered in a hurry, and Sting was simply not in a hurry.

His black singlet usually had a white scorpion down the side, calling to his finishing move—the Scorpion Deathlock. I'd often let my brother perform multiple Figure-Fours, Lion Tamers, or Texas Cloverleafs if I could try just one Scorpion Deathlock. He'd usually opt for Lex Luger's Torture Rack or Scott Hall's Outsider's Edge. My body was too limber at the time to care.

The problem with seeing Sting in Shreveport was he'd disappeared earlier that season. His unexplained absence lent well to his loner-persona, and now reeks of the innocence of 1990s television. Today—I haven't seen a wrestling match in over twenty years—I'd imagine each wrestler is milked for their shelf-life then discarded. No more slow burns.

Whatever the reason for the absence (according to a Reddit forum, it was so he could grow his hair longer and might've had a baby—WCW on the cutting edge of paternity leave), the chances of him reemerging in Shreveport were low.

As far as I knew, kids from Shreveport weren't allowed to watch wrestling anyway—my cousins there hadn't heard of Sting, and my aunt made me turn it off one summer night the year before because it was too violent. Some things are too real for Shreveport and other places still shedding the veneer of the old south's counterfeit ornateness.

I don't remember much about the drive there, but the orange-clad security guards waving glowing batons and checking tickets out of windows in the dusty field of a parking lot is a scene I've seen before and since. The arena, a converted hockey rink for the amateur team the Mud Bugs, was a glorified barn.

I didn't blink for an hour. Chris Jericho ran in for a match with Ultimo Dragon. Jericho, a perpetual heel, locked him in a Lion Tamer much to the chagrin of the ArkLaTex fanbase. He ran around the ring, an exaggerated look of sincere confusion across his face, and stormed off petulantly to boos he'd just whipped up. Masterful.

There was a tag team match, which meant the Harlem Heat were involved. They kicked their way to a win against Scott Hall and Kevin Nash. Nash was so large that he simply stepped over the top rope while the others (not including lightweights that flipped over) bent under to get in the ring.

A pair of older guys behind us kept pointing to the rafters and shouting "Sting!" They got me every time and spilled their beers with each laugh. Cale's dad, a high school baseball coach, eventually turned around to tell them to knock it off, and they bought him a beer instead.

Somewhere around the fifth undercard fight, I got up to go to the bathroom. Walking along the dark, musty concourse to the urinal trough, I saw a vendor with a bouquet of blinking red roses. My mom had given me ten dollars for the trip. That wasn't near enough to buy a shirt or Sting mask, but it was enough for this plastic flower. This was before the merchandise apparel industry really took off, or at least not every fan in the crowd of a football or baseball game felt inclined to wear a jersey or team-sponsored shirt in the 90s. You'd see people in white t-shirts and jeans before Nike figured out what it had been missing.

I had the urge to buy something to commemorate the trip, and this might placate my mom's feelings about wrestling—look, they have nice fake roses that perpetually smell like the vendor's gas station cologne. The rose glowed in my hand when I found my way back to my seat a few minutes later.

Diamond Dallas Page got somebody with the Diamond Cutter. His curly blond mullet bounced around his neck as he showed off his patented diamond symbol to each corner of the arena. If I remember nothing on my death bed, I'll remember Goldberg's spear from that night in the final fight. The stadium, damp and cool like they thought the Mud Bugs were playing, erupting. Some people throwing plastic roses on the mat during the ref's triple count.

When we got back, sometime late at night, I went to my parents' bedroom and thanked my mom for letting me go, displaying the red rose only to find the batteries went out on the ride home. She had her eye makeup off and was rubbing Vaseline on her pale cheeks, so I could see exactly how surprised she was by the rose before she put it in a drawer and sent me to bed.

I sat blinking at my bedroom ceiling. It was fake alright, but that didn't stop it from being awesome.

I don't know what's become of those wrestlers. Sting eventually came back and joined an outfit of villains—the NWO—and I settled back to Juventud and Eddie. The last I saw of Hulk Hogan he was getting sued by his daughter, and Diamond Dallas Page was on Shark Tank peddling yoga DVDs.

They've been shoved in a drawer.

Except for Dwayne "The Rock" Johnson, Dave Bautista, and John Cena… but those are WWF guys, so a tad gauche for my household.

Frontier Psychiatry

One evening my dad stood on a rickety deck attached to a ranch he'd rented for our family vacation in Wyoming for his seventieth birthday. There were chickens, goats, and two young ranch hands whose dad owned the place—he'd been a Gucci model, my dad explained after one of my sister's third or fourth remarks about how attractive the ranch hands were. They were both tall and lean but had total capacity over all their joints, unlike some European NBA prospect you see achingly wobble up to the stage on draft night. These two had played soccer, wiffleball, and kickball with us all week without the slightest hint of arthritic collapse. For that reason, they were unlike the men in our family, or at least my brother and I—both on the shorter and academic end of the student-athlete bridge.

The ranch house itself was expansive but weary in all the wrong places. First, my dad did his usual huff and gruff call to order, sniffling and scratching his mustache with his index finger. Then, holding out a can of Miller Lite, he proposed a toast. Two days before his birthday was my parents' forty-eighth wedding anniversary, and, looking out on the table of eleven adults—my siblings and I plus our spouses and our mother—he rambled through a short soliloquy that I've always known only he can get away with: "It's so great having everyone here together, watching me get closer to the dirt nap I'll take soon. And for our forty-eighth anniversary, too, it's been fun… like getting pecked to death by a duck every day for forty-eight years."

ꝏ

My kids had never flown before, so we packed every Dora and Disney item we could lay our hands on and hoped for the best. After a slight hiccup at the American Airlines bag check station, where they insisted I check my own bags while also insisting I was doing it wrong, the trip went smoothly. The waiter at the Dallas airport's TGIFriday's called me "boss" several times, so I was in high spirits when we arrived in Jackson, Wyoming.

My dad was supposed to pick us up. I walked down the tarmac, breathing in what my kids called "little air" because it seemed like a diet compared to the thick swamp oxygen they're used to. I called my dad to see if he was there yet. Not yet—on a beer run, but he'd be there by the time we got our bags, he said. He and my mom started a tradition a few years back where they'd take each grandkid on a trip of their choosing when the kid turned nine. That year, three grandkids turned nine, so they took the trio to Yellowstone a week before this trip to kill two birds with one flight. I figured my dad could use a beer run after a week in a car with my mom and three nine-year-olds.

We walked out a short time later into the calmness of a parking lot that only a regional airport could provide. My hometown, Texarkana, has one of those airports where you walk from your car up to the plane, and so was Jackson's, so I figured maybe Texarkana is turning the corner into quaint.

My dad was standing against our black rental Toyota, his white legs looking like he swapped them with a cadaver, and his gray shorts-pants combo unzipped above the knee so the pants portion dangled to his ankles.

We pulled out, stopping for only a moment so he could open a beer and we could look at a cowboy statue for my son to yell, "Cowboy!" He learned the word from a Kid Rock song I played for a while before a western-themed engagement party we hosted at high noon one Saturday a month before.

"So," I said, "how's your trip been?"

"I'm thinking about going home. So that's how it's been," he said, laughing. Melissa cracked up from the back, giggling at what she knew would be a story.

"Every night, ev-er-y night," he said, letting go of the wheel and waving with both hands like he was washing the side of a double-decker bus and taking a swig out of the shimmering can, "every night when we were settling down, your mom, Mamalise," he said, looking back to my kids so they'd understand the full grasp of the setting. "Mamalise would ask the kids what their high of the day was and what their low of the day was. High and low. And Jimmy," my sister Leigh's son, "he'd about had enough of Tommy and Olivia, so he said, 'those two,' and pointed at 'em for his low." Tommy and Olivia are my sister Katie's set of twins.

"Well, Tommy didn't have much to say. You know he likes to pick at people, so he would say something about Jimmy. And then Olivia, sheesh!" Olivia, who turned nine on the trip, was the most emotionally mature person in the house that first week and probably the second. "Olivia, every night, said her high was something or another—horses or something, you know kids. But her low, she'd look at me out of the corner of those eyes," he said as he cracked open another beer, "and say, 'My low was Daddy-O's attitude! Then, then I'd say, well, mine was *your* attitude! And your mother would step in. Then, 'Dennis!' she'd start yelling. So, you know, we had fun." He smiled and took a sip, balancing the can on his bare knee, both hands on the wheel.

Melissa was in the back of the car, pointing out mountains and the big sky to my four and two-year-olds, Flannery and Henry. We'd turn a bend in the road, and the sky would grow, stretching beyond the range and river up to the foot of mountains capped with pearly snow like cupcakes. The ski runs sliced through the trees near Jackson like a lawn mower had run them over in smooth tracks straight out of the clouds. The gondolas looked like little blue baskets teetering up the side.

"Flan," my dad turned to look at my daughter buckled into her travel car seat, "those mountains are called the Grand Tetons, it means *Big Breasts* in French. Oh, damn," he said, looking at me with all the care in the world, "she probably doesn't even know what French means yet, right?"

My dad isn't immune to the plight of many men his age. Some of his quips are suited less for writing and more for a deposition testimony where his colloquial defense can be spun into a more formidable web than "You can't say that shit anymore?"

He was always one of those people, one of those dads at least, that my friends would ask—*Where is your dad? Is your dad coming? Your dad going to be there?* And, with a knowing grin, *what's your dad been up to?* They could've met him once, twice, or grown up with me; either way, there's no chance he remembers their name except for a couple he assigned nicknames based on physical attributes wholly unrelated to the person. My college buddy Nick, for instance, has brown wavy hair, a beard, was a groomsman in my wedding, and my dad still calls him "that blonde curly-headed shit." And my best man—other than my dad—my friend Worm. His real name is Jarrod, but my dad still thinks his nickname is another insect like a caterpillar or dragonfly because, to an objective mind, those are both better than Worm. Dad is still worried about Worm suing us after I hit him in the left ear with a Titleist, causing partial deafness and partially free law school tuition that he has yet to thank me for. I don't know what the statute of limitations are on that kind of crime because I went to law school at LSU.

As I look at my life now, particularly regarding the type of father I want to be, I'm optimistic that plenty of people ask about my whereabouts over my two-year-old son Henry. And my dad's best friend goes by Weird, so we have multiple things in common.

My dad is the type of guy that woke up early on Christmas morning to put beer out for the garbagemen having to work on those southern sleet-filled mornings. Coors light, mountains blue, and lately, a Christmas IPA—an unfortunate side effect of my brother's medical residency in Portland, Oregon. My dad's the type of guy that was a cross-country cattle driver, a trucker with the radio signal "Fox Squirrel" during the years between college and med school acceptance. He's the type of guy who got along with me during my younger years because I liked his favorite sport: baseball. And, as he said during his speech at my rehearsal dinner, I was okay at it. Baseball kept us close until he was my coach one summer and introduced the nickname "Slow-Banion" to my teammates.

He's the type of guy that once owned two Hummers. One white; one yellow. He tucked one away under a car cover behind our dog kennels around the back driveway so he could have a fresh Hummer when his current one crapped out. He's the type of guy that's owned a GTO, a Corvette, a Porsche, and a Ferrari and promptly sold all of them (multiple to the goalie of the Chicago Blackhawks) after "getting them up as fast as they'd go," as he told me. He took the Ferrari and me down near the bottoms of Texarkana, where there's a straightaway and a slight graded turn, and I got it up to 155 miles an hour. He was beside me the whole time, drinking a beer, saying, "Isn't this great? It never even shakes!" I shook—like a dog shitting razor blades— too nervous to breathe. He's the type of guy who when we needed a lawnmower part, he'd send me across a moldy wooden bridge to the neighbors' abandoned garage to start picking through it. They returned after a few years' hiatus, and he blamed all their missing items on me. He told my friend Carter—a classical baritone performing in my sister Katie's wedding—that he hoped Carter enjoyed the gift they got him for singing the Latin version of Ave Maria because my dad, as he said, "had been with women that cost less than that whiskey." All this while holding Katie's arm in the crook of his elbow, seconds before Canon in D broke the moment. My dad hired him for the wedding after Carter and I had evacuated to Texarkana during Hurricane Gustav. We met my parents at a Mexican restaurant where Carter got drunk on margaritas and sang happy birthday to our dentist. Curly-headed Nick was there too but not as loud.

My dad is the type of guy that went on a golf trip to Scotland only for Sean Connery to dribble a ball in his fairway. Instead of playing through, Connery insisted my dad go first. Then, in front of James Bond, my dad hit what he called a "piss missile" to the green. James Bond said, "Great shot, Laddie. Great shot."

He's the type of guy that called me the other day, stopped mid-sentence, hacked, then said, "Shit, I almost just exasperated on a pork rind ..."

He's the type of guy whose father loaned him five thousand dollars at twenty percent interest when he went to med school. Twenty percent because his dad told him he was a bad bet. His dad later gifted him a shotgun at his medical school graduation, and my dad is the type of guy that could tell just by looking at this shotgun stuffed in a garbage bag, serial number scratched to hell, that it was stolen. He's the type of guy who still calls me to tell me how quickly he got his Ferrari to Atlanta, Texas, where he goes weekly to treat a small farming community outside of Texarkana. He was a surgeon, a college baseball player, a lumber mill worker in high school, and once got me out of jail because he operated on the officer's mother's gallbladder.

He's proud of the fact that he was the first white person in his hometown to invite a black person to their wedding, but he's the type of guy that still makes me nervous in the Popeye's drive thru. I'm still not entirely sure where he stands on most political issues. Still, he's the type of guy that asked my brother's gay buddy Coleman if he'd ever had a water enema because, in his words, "I'm about to scatter your ass across that water" right before he revved the engine of a pontoon boat. Coleman clung to a wabbling neon innertube then responded, "Don't ask what you don't wanna know, Dennis," and my dad's the type of guy that was more excited by that response than when I introduced him to my son Henry Dennis.

ꝏ

If it seems I mentioned med school or the profession often, it's because that's the only career my family currently understands. My dad, brother, sister-in-law, and one brother-in-law all practice medicine. When I worked as a nursing home administrator for two years—a glorified Medicaid pusher—my dad would call to chat about the business and compare it to his years as a chief surgery resident. On another family vacation a few years before, my dad went around the room to tell us how proud he was of everyone. "Who would have thought I'd sire a doctor, who married a doctor, the wife of a doctor, and ..." surveying the rest of the room, "a stripper!" pointing to my wife, who works in advertising. Melissa and I were the only ones laughing, knowing good and well that a stripper makes more money than we do.

That week at the Wyoming ranch, he'd get drunk and discuss his dad's inability to appreciate his career or express emotion. My dad is the type of guy that ends every phone conversation with "love you," then waits for your response before adding, "You know how many times my dad said that to me?"

"Not one damn time," we say in unison around a fire in Wyoming.

The last time I saw my grandfather before his open casket funeral was in Monticello, Arkansas, where he was held up with my dad's sister and her three boys. The boys all earned some form of an athletic scholarship to the University of Arkansas before losing them in their own unique way—one got too drunk at Señor Frogs in Cancún the week before a state All-Star game that led to seven errors. Hell of a hangover.

My dad drove me the two hours from Texarkana to Monticello for a weekend during my sophomore year of high school. Poppa, who lived with us until he refused to clean his cigarette ashes off the back porch, was in hog heaven in Monticello. The three boys rode four-wheelers, fished in a pond they'd dug in the back, and chewed tobacco all day while their mom, my aunt Nel, cooked things like smothered pork chops and gravy out of the galley kitchen. My uncle Hoyt ran the Napa store in town and cleaned up Poppa's cigarette butts at night.

I'd gone to interview him for a family lineage project that, so far, I only had a few articles about a former gangster with a whiff of relation to my dad and a former Texas President on my mom's side. Poppa wore a blue plaid shirt, voluminous khaki pants, and black orthopedic shoes. Squished into a creaky folding chair on the porch, he smoked like he hoped to expire mid-interview.

"He was a gunner in World War Two," I told my dad on the drive home.

"Bull-shit," my dad said, flicking his cigarette out the Hummer's window. "Well, maybe he was, but he never told me that. Never told me he loved me either."

ꕤ

The ranch was a red clack board barn on a gravel-lined hill. Wood paneling and puckered green carpet filled the twelve thousand square feet, as well as an assortment of mounted antlers and pirate memorabilia. One piece of wood—that the TripAdvisor listing claimed came directly off a pirate mast—hung over the red felt pool table and wobbled back and forth when the porch doors were open at night to allow for some airflow. My dad called it Frontier Air Conditioning more than once. A mermaid with a bow and arrow sat proudly on the edge of the plank, just in swinging distance for one of my nephews to smack it with a pool cue on the first night, snapping the arrowhead clean off. Seven of the eleven boys ran shirtless through the house with the broken arrowhead above their heads before my brother snagged it and crammed it into one of the fifty wooden kitchen drawers.

There were three floors, and all seven bedrooms had a unique theme. As for me and mine, we stayed in the third-floor room with a balcony overlooking the goat field. The theme of our room was, for a brief period, stifling heat. There wasn't an A/C in the house until I opened a hallway closet on the second day, found a window unit air conditioner, and had Rex install it in our room. It was, by my account, my finest hour on the trip and as a father in general. My sister Katie and her husband Steve stayed in the frontier room. My sister Mary Claire and her husband Brent stayed in the aspen suite with aspen tree bark on the walls. My brother David and his wife Jacquelyn slept in the other upstairs room, the leather room, until retreating to the downstairs guest with no discernable theme—victims of the first night's heat. My sister Leigh and her husband James have seven kids, so I never got the nerve to see where they were staying or what they were doing. My parents were in the master, which had another fireplace, another elk, a bear rug, and a jacuzzi tub we used to bathe the smaller grandkids each night. Lathering them and spraying them down together.

The front door came off a gravel driveway, and we usually ran in with one of the seven goats not far behind. Unfortunately, I missed the memo on day one that if you touch a goat's horn, it thinks you want to play, and they play by ramming their skull into your midsection. So, after petting a black and white speckled goat's horn, wondering what precisely a goat's horn felt like, I had to use one of the many baby strollers on the front porch as a makeshift riot shield, throwing it at the goat and scrambling in the glass door.

Inside, the kitchen counter encircled an old stove that sat cattycorner to a fireplace with an enormous elk hanging overhead. My mom tinkered with the oven the first night when we had frozen lasagna and frozen garlic bread, and that's how we found out the gas leaked, so we avoided the kitchen except for Wednesday's fajita night and if we wanted to nap.

The dining room had a long table made from a single piece of oak which pointed into the TV room—a room with a leather couch and a TV. These two opened into what we called the living room.

The living room was a sprawling bastion of roadside knickknacks. There were wooden blocks, guitars, crystal glassware, the pool table, couches, and chairs encapsulating every form of feng shui, and more elk. In the evenings, we'd put a white box fan at the western wall of open doors, and a hint of cool air rolled in, filling the house as the shadows lengthened across the red felt, the brown elk fur, and the molding pirate wood.

Outside the living room, through the wall of glass doors, was the main porch. The warped boards bowed and bent when you walked to the edge, and the table and chairs almost bounced in place when you sat down. Out there we ate, drank, and acquiesced to my brother David and youngest sister Mary Claire's deranged desires to play a chorus line of board games.

The property itself was worth whatever my dad paid for it, the rest of us agreed. There was a field large enough for a jet landing, a barn full of mostly non-threatening livestock, and to the east, a skeleton of a tepee sat with a chandelier hung over a fire pit, and all of this slipped under groves of aspen trees and mountain peaks.

Rex showed me a small pump well sticking up near the chicken coops. He said it came directly from an underground spring and would be the freshest, coldest water I'd ever tasted. Of course, he didn't know I lived in Baton Rouge, which has the second cleanest drinking water in the country, so I told him all about it before mockingly sipping from a spout with water so clear and cold that I'd swear it improved my eyesight by the end of the week.

One of the last nights, Flannery stood in her light pink nightgown, the setting sun glowing through her light brown hair, drinking a glass of the well water, and asked me why we couldn't stay.

"Oh, man. What did you tell her?" Melissa asked later.

"I said, you remember when daddy said we can't go into the Target store because it's too expensive? This whole place is one big Target store. But no pretzels."

ꕥ

The first morning my mom called a head of households meeting. The week before, she'd instructed us via text to nominate one person to be the head of household. They would attend meetings and make decisions on our behalf. I nominated Melissa. Melissa nominated Melissa, too.

My parents have a clear pecking order for their children's spouses, one whose middle is up for some debate, but the top is written into stone tablets: Melissa. I think Melissa is great for a myriad of reasons, but my parents like her most because she once told me I was grumpy at a dinner in New Orleans before she ran off and passed out in the Windsor Court bathroom.

The head of households met around the oak table, crammed against the walls and cabernet red upholstered wooden chairs. I made a quick stop to dispel any rumors that, yes, I had indeed found a window unit that morning and had Rex install it. And I watched him drill it into the foundation, so don't try me. Then I took off, knowing Mel had more important matters to discuss, namely the Instacart order.

My mom was red in the face, staring blankly at the agenda she'd written that morning, and she looked at me over her reading glasses in a way that hurried my feet. She was excited about this trip and didn't need any distractions.

During the pandemic, my mom called almost daily. It had been just her, my dad, and the dogs for over a decade, but 2020 was an isolating year for everyone, let alone someone tucked behind the pine curtain of East Texas. She called more after someone floated the idea of Wyoming for their seventieth birthdays. She'd call and check on dates, times, food allergies, updated ETAs, and political party affiliations. I think she secretly hoped that the structure of the head-of-household meetings might provide the path of least political resistance within the ranks.

We, as in my entire immediate family, hadn't been together since my wedding in Shreveport in the summer of 2016 when, according to multiple sources, one of my brothers-in-law pulled a gun on another at the rehearsal dinner. On the top floor of Shreveport's downtown Petroleum Club (a tan-carpeted ballroom with pane-glass walls overlooking the city), the power flickering during a thunderstorm, and if I hadn't been preoccupied with fitting into an old seersucker suit, I might've noticed the game of Clue unfolding. Everyone involved claims no weapons were formally introduced, but the truth is somewhere in the middle. The argument had bloomed and blossomed over either politics or college football. Two of my sisters and their husbands were staunch republicans, hanging a George Washington painting over the mantle. More religious than right-wing, probably, these were the sisters with five and seven children.

One, Leigh, went to the University of Texas, where she met her husband, James. They got married the summer after their college graduation, and a group of my friends performed as gentlemen dancers at her bachelorette party, something James didn't fully appreciate until recently—one had borrowed a real fireman's uniform from his dad. The other pulled off an almost perfect Risky Business slide. Their seven kids—Susie, Jack, Jimmy, Luke, Matthew, Paul, and Mary Margaret—acted better in church than I did.

My oldest sister and sibling, Katie, went to Notre Dame, where she read at masses. Her husband Steve, a self-made ER surgeon who, from what I've pieced together, lived with his parents in an RV most of his life, was in the national guard and our family's only tenable connection to the military despite my dad wishing I'd tried JAG in law school. I was too lazy to look up the physical requirements. Steve had a "NObama" sticker on his Jeep at my wedding. Her five kids were Nick and Jacob, two stepsons from Steve's previous marriage, an eleven-year-old Ellie, and the set of twins Tommy and Olivia.

My Atlanta siblings, David and Mary Claire, sat with their spouses on the other side of the table. David went to LSU and studied English before becoming a pediatrician. He voted for Obama. He wore Heely shoes around the hospital, rolling into kids' rooms while he checked their charts and recommended no more juice—like he told me on our road trip from San Antonio to his residency in Portland. David picked out a book I should have read for each stop, inscribing the inside with "Books English Majors Should Read," and would hand me Vonnegut or McCarthy on our stops in Sedona, Arizona, or Humboldt, California. He slapped the shit out of me for trying to piss near a redwood's root system in northern California. His wife, Jacquelyn, went to Wake Forrest, so she wasn't as aggressive in the college football discussions. She used to figure skate with Tara Lipinksi and routinely left the US to operate on kids' eyes. They'd lived in Portland, Oklahoma City, London, and Atlanta. When they named their son Otis, my mom's cousin in Baton Rouge, whom we called Aunt Lynn, almost keeled over laughing, asking if the kid was black. Aunt Lynn had insomnia and watched the news on a small bubble TV on the kitchen counter, rabbit ear antennas rising to the ceiling with the smoke of one of her Virginia Slims lying in an LSU ashtray. She didn't vote for Obama but loves David.

Mary Claire went to Texas, then to graduate school at Notre Dame, where she met her husband and Fighting Irish apologist Brent. They both taught in underprivileged private schools in Denver, which I assumed was an oxymoron, before moving to Atlanta, where MC teaches at a school on a body of water with kids whose parents own companies you've heard of.

She's still adjusting to the heat. They almost named their first kid "Blaise" after a saint canonized for his work as a physician, which would've scored points with my dad. "Right?" My mom said on the phone when she felt my face contorting after she told me the name Blaise. Instead, they landed on Lewis, who they like to mockingly say "has all the confidence of a white male," and then Elodie for their daughter, who turned one a few weeks before the Wyoming trip. Brent's family talks about Notre Dame football like we're still in the 80s, and David and I had to apologize after our wedding toast disparaged their coach, who is now at our alma mater.

Melissa and I landed somewhere in the middle. We were probably the only ones on the trip without a hardline stance on abortion, and I hadn't voted in any elections since I ran for secretary of my high school senior class.

Sitting around the teepee fire pit the first night in Wyoming, there was a bit of a sizing-up ceremony. Full of frozen Stouffer's lasagna, kids in bed, and goats encircling the chopped log stools and creaking iron benches, everyone drank and listened while James played a Neutral Milk Hotel song on the guitar from the living room while Steve pulled out a travel guitar he'd been picking on. Leigh provided percussion, periodically smacking a goat away with her book.

My dad, multiple drinks ahead, felt it a good time to bring up James' dad's passing a few years before, then steered into college football again, both death and college football polite fire conversation in the south.

Then he told us how much he loved us enough that we thought he might be next to go.

"Dad," Katie said, shaking her head, "Is everything okay? Jeez."

"I just wanted to say it. My daddy never told me," Dad said.

"Oh, yes he did, Dennis," Mom said. "I didn't know you played guitar, James?"

Having a conversation in my family was like a game of Battleship. You'd lob out a topic, and the first one to hit another person and catch their attention went to work on finding the rest.

"Yeah," he said, "I don't know if I really play, but I know a couple of songs. I picked it up in the pandemic last year sometime, and it's been a good time waster."

"I still remember dropping all of you off at college. Do you think my daddy went with me to college?"

"Dennis, you went to college two miles from your parent's front door."

"Still… do you think he ever came?"

"What other songs you got, James?" David asked.

"Do we have anything planned for tomorrow?" Melissa asked.

"Katie," my dad said, his eyes blinking from the cloud of smoke gurgling off the fire, "do you remember when I took you to Notre Dame, and you…."

"And you made me steal apples from orientation breakfast in the dining hall?"

My dad shut his eyes and slapped his knee. "And you ran out with a few under your arm. That's how you save money, I told you!"

"That was so embarrassing," she said, smiling and breathing in, eyes wide. "There I was at Notre Dame, thinking I had really made it. There are priests and professors everywhere, and dad is in the corner scheming on the best way to get free apples into the dorm room."

"Leigh used to steal tampons at the Harvard Law Library," James said.

"Well," Leigh said, swirling a glass of red wine, "they had the Pearl tampons there! Just in a basket in the women's room. If I walked in like I knew what I was doing, nobody ever asked."

"Because you're white," a member of the Atlanta cohort chimed in. This would be a mainstay of theirs on a trip where there were fewer minorities than mountain peaks. Coming from Louisiana to Wyoming is jarring for multiple reasons—the well-paved roads, the clean air, and the homogeneous skin tones hiding under Patagonia hats.

"Probably," Leigh said, shrugging, "But when you're bleeding and don't have enough money, it doesn't matter how you got one. I wanted one of those Pearl ones, not the cardboard ones we could afford."

I sat on a stump, shivering from the image and the night air coming through the trees. Melissa and I went up to bed after my mom told us how her mother knew Katie and Mary Claire were more fertile than Leigh—they had hair on their face.

"That wasn't so bad," I said, climbing the lumpy stairs to our whirring window unit room.

"You are so dramatic," Melissa said. "Nothing is going to happen."

"David is an inch away from bringing up January 6th, you just watch, or the 2019 LSU-Texas game. One of the two."

◦

The next day we piled into our four rental cars (one blue Toyota Sequoia, two black Ford Extended Expeditions, and one white fifteen-person passenger van) and headed for a hike.

My kids got naked at the first sign of water, and others ran into the clear, still pond on the inside of the walking path. We lugged a toddler carrier hiking backpack through airport security, so I wasn't going to not use it. I strapped a wet and cold Henry down for the half-mile stroll before he finally got his diaper entirely off.

"This is fun," everyone repeated when a kid would go momentarily missing, like when Lewis waded too far into the water, losing his footing and floundering before Brent sprinted in to save him. "White male confidence!" they said of Lewis, I think meaning he feels he can accomplish anything.

The pond sat on the opposite side of a rock levy from the Snake River. We ran up the hill to see it rush by, and I gripped Henry's hand tight. Something about Lewis running into the pond and the sheer noise of the river made me appreciate the opportunity for disaster. I looked at Henry like I would the next day in a gondola, and the next in Yellowstone National Park, and the next when he watched his cousin Jimmy catch one of the chickens—he was seeing something for the first time, and I'd finally discovered why parents take their toddlers to Disney World. He probably won't remember this moment, the first time he saw a real river, not the standing line of drainage near our house in Louisiana, but I won't soon forget it.

My mom, checking her watch, called us back to the cars. We needed to get home and rest before that night.

⚭

They must've come from all over the country. From Los Angeles, Denver, Boston, or maybe just Cheyenne. Moths to the artistic flame. Actors, musicians, country western minstrels, and trained horseback riders were all willing to lay down their pride for Flippin' Willie's Chuck Wagon Dinner Theater and Band show.

Despite his years as a cattle truck driver, my dad had shed any trappings of a frontier lifestyle besides a handlebar mustache and occasional *Paint Your Wagon* reference. However, he made an exception tonight and dressed in his brightest blue jeans, brown boots, and a pearl snap shirt my mom got him from Academy Sports in Texarkana. His hat was more Indiana Jones than Oregon Trail, and he flipped me the bird when I suggested as much.

After unloading the cars, we made our way into a waiting area shaped like a large stable, restless but ready for the chuck dinner. There were memorials of either cowboys or actors on the wall. "Bean Sprout" Thompson and Barry "Brass" Herrington, and an old black and white photo with a disheveled, plump man staring back at me.

"That's Nick Wilson," an unfamiliar twangy voice said behind me.

I turned to see a man in his mid-to-late fifties towering over me. He reminded me, probably because I'd been inundated with Disney movies, of the Sherriff of Nottingham from the cartoon Robin Hood. The scruff around his chin was a feral blend of brown and red, making his black mop of hair look dyed. His salt-stained white shirt gave off the appearance he'd just come from work. A nice touch.

"If you say so," I said.

"He founded Wilson."

"You don't say," I said, leaning to almost bump noses with the portrait. I'd tried one of Rex's special candies that I suspect altered my state because I was close enough to give Uncle Nick an Eskimo kiss (a phrase an Atlanta sibling rolled their eyes at, but I still can't find a more succinct, universal way of saying).

"Alright, folks!" the man behind me yelled, "It's time to get movin'!"

The family piled into a covered wagon towed by two horses that the high school-aged girl driving the wagon told us were named Johnny and June. We trudged over a few hills, passing mountain bikers and even a car along the way. Eventually, an outlaw sprung from the woods on a paint horse, screaming we'd better get outta there quick before his posse showed up. He had a raccoon skin hat and a red cotton shirt that showed the pools of sweat from sitting under the emaciated shade of an aspen tree.

My nephew Tommy, in a perfect example of his generation either needing more to raise the needle after the bombardment of entertainment available to them now or just someone that doesn't appreciate the finer points of local theater, called the man a nerd as he rode to the next wagon.

"Well, that's at least good to see," Mary Claire said. "Last time we came, they had someone dressed up like a Native American."

The dinner line consisted of a green salad with the option of ranch or Russian dressing ladled onto your leaves, barbeque beans plopped next to the salad, and a form of meat I wasn't familiar with. It came with a roll and a brownie, and a gluten-free brownie for my nephew Jimmy, who was as slender as a pipe cleaner.

The show started with The Devil Went Down to Jackson and ended three hours later with a prayer. Yellow jackets swarmed the sticky pools of sugar under the lemonade stand near our table, and a cloud of dust blew in every time an outlaw rode by.

I left a mark on Flannery's arm when we went to the Port-A-Potty in the middle of the show. The door swung open to a blue drum turned upside down with a small sconce on the side and a little brown lid that, when I opened, appeared to lead to another dimension. A dark, rotting dimension without sight or love. I held her wrist like I'd break it before letting her go, all the while, she tried breathing out of her mouth because of the smell.

When we returned to the table, most of the dinner plates cleared as people moved on to dessert. I was sitting near Jacquelyn, facing the stage. Most of the kids ran out to a nearby creek as the band played an array of somber Church tunes.

"Do you see this?" Jacquelyn asked, pointing to the table in front of us where all the grandkids had been sitting.

There was Tommy, who was slowly moving up my list of favorite relatives, eyeing his parents like the Mona Lisa before swiping one brownie after another from the top of the picnic table. He'd tear open the cellophane wrapper and have each dark square down in two bites. Before long, he'd made his way around the table to the big light brown square that was the gluten-free brownie cake.

"Tommy," Katie said, a marathon runner in her own right, "You know that I can see you, right?"

"I just wanted to see if they tasted the same!" He said before scooting off to the creek.

It was agreed that while different from the other seventeen or so grandkids, Tommy will be on the cover of a tech magazine one day holding up a vial of something, possibly an edible gluten-free brownie.

This isn't a disaster story. Everyone was so busy planning their own escape that it turned into everyone wanting to run off together.

Wednesday, we went to town and rode on an alpine slide—a concrete path you slide down on a rickety old bobsled—we'd all gone down as kids. We ponied up for a couple of all-day passes and switched the bracelets around while the zonked-out college kids let us through the turnstiles over and over for hours on end.

We took a gondola up to the top of a mountain and had corn dogs and beers, Flannery and Henry getting their first taste of my fear of heights and canned nacho cheese.

My friend Corey used to point out how strange it was that my family was spread across the country. Texarkana, Denver, Houston, Dallas, Baton Rouge, and Atlanta. And, more so, how strange our relationship was. Corey has two half-siblings that he often sees, either them coming to Baton Rouge for his son's birthday parties or him going home to Mobile to see their mom and dad. "Do y'all hate each other? Or just never say you love each other?"

If a sibling of mine looked at me across a dinner table and said they loved me, I think my gut would be disappointed. Yeah, let's hope so, I'd think. We used to yell good night from our respective rooms upstairs at home. A regular Mick-Yankee Von Trapp family. It was like a family full of friends—your relationships ebbing and flowing. Sometimes intense, like when Mary Claire voluntarily gave up her computer time so I could get on AOL and talk to girls, but sometimes ramming headfirst into a dam built by COVID vaccine syringes. It's not that we didn't love each other, we just didn't say it much—we get that from our paternal grandfather, so I hear.

We had family pictures that evening where the tattooed photographer and I marveled at the regimented discipline of Leigh's seven children.

We went to Yellowstone the next day, an eight-hour car ride where we drew straws to see who had to join Leigh's family in the fifteen-passenger van. It was decided the night before that I would drive all of the grandkids in the van, and the rest of the adults would go alone. I sobered up in the morning and grabbed the Toyota for my family, and we sped off through Grand Teton National Park and into Yellowstone.

Henry promptly stole a baseball with a buffalo on it from a gift outpost near Old Faithful, and Flannery wanted goldfish instead of the peanut butter and jelly sandwiches we'd packed. We saw the geysers rise and fall, and I bought a slew of stickers to put on a water bottle knowing it would annoy Melissa. Henry laughed and screamed when a buffalo lodged itself between our car and the road, the bison snorting and stamping while Henry kicked my chair back in his purest expression of excitement. David, driving one of the black Expeditions, claims he saw a bear on the top of the loop we all drove. The rest of his car was asleep.

It was my fifth time in Yellowstone and the first time since Worm and I blew through a few years before without seeing one scruff of buffalo or elk. He was focused mainly on the Tinder profiles of the park rangers. Back in Baton Rouge, we've now been to Buffalo Wild Wings more than I'd like to admit so Henry can look at the taxidermized art hanging in the lobby.

"Gondola, daddy," he says each time.

"Sure thing, buddy," I say each time. The closest thing to mountains in Baton Rouge are the Indian burial mounds on LSU's campus, and they fenced those off a few years ago after allowing decades of cardboard sled races down the banks. Henry squeezed through one time and ran up the grassy hill. White male confidence.

ꝏ

We bumped along the tram tracks to our gate at the Dallas airport a few days later. Flannery and Henry holding stuffed buffalo and fox toys, respectively, and Melissa bracing herself with a steel pole hanging from the ceiling—finally giving in to the stripper moniker my dad gave her. We could feel the Texas heat seeping through the cracks of the doors, the sun seemed to be a little closer here than in Wyoming.

I thought about the grass on the ranch lawn. It's impressive how comfortable someone can get when the weather isn't trying to kill you, and there's no threat of snakes around. I fell asleep under an aspen tree a couple of times on the trip. Once waking up to the whack of a wiffleball bat, another time to Flannery butt-naked with face paint all over her stomach and legs—her face painted like a pink fox, her nose an inch from mine, and her asking me to stop snoring. The last time I woke up in the grass was the hollow pop of wooden figures hitting each other.

David and Brent were playing a yard game that I'd only seen one other time, and the people playing looked so happy and sober that I asked if they were Mormon—they were.

That final night was my dad's birthday. It also happened to be Henry's second birthday and Tommy and Olivia's ninth birthday. I don't know what the sexual occasion was for the others involved, but Henry is a result of Joe Burrow beating Alabama in 2019.

Tommy got busted going through the presents earlier in the day, checking to make sure everyone got the same amount, and there was a brief squabble over the culpability and capability of a nine-year-old to show restraint. My dad had been on the trip for two weeks and was at the end of whatever frayed rope he'd flown up with, staring straight forward, chewing the steak James added to the Instacart order in the eleventh hour.

"What was everyone's high and low on the trip?" my mom asked.

"Oh, not this again, Malise," my dad said, dropping his bread onto his plate.

Katie, who had moved her family to Boise right before the pandemic, geographically severing any direct flight paths back to the rest of us, hung her head. I was nine when Katie went to college—her the oldest, me the youngest—and I barely remember what her room looked like before Leigh moved in and painted it purple with a blotchy sponge that was fashionable in the early 2000s. Her oldest stepson went to LSU for a couple of semesters before leaving for the military—the last time I saw him was at a bar with a girl with boobs bigger than my head. I called Katie to update her. "It looks like he's doing great—making some great friends!" He'd drop out a couple of weeks later, so that was always on my mind, wondering if Katie wanted me to help more than I had, knowing full well she didn't. Her path led her back to Dallas before our trip to Wyoming, and it was the first time I'd seen her since Flannery was born, and she drove eight hours to come to be with us.

Her eyes were red and swollen when she looked up from the table. "I just can't," she said. "I just had the best time."

The sun was in its first move toward the mountain peaks on our last night, right at the level to shine on the wooden white Adirondack chairs lined up next to the first-base line.

There were shrieking, curdling, gulping, bleating cries combined with hurried shouts and panting. And clucks. The patchy green property flowed down a hill into a white fence leading to an elk preserve at the foot of Wyoming's Teton mountain range. My brother-in-law Steve got drunk at one point and hopped the white fence hoping for some headspace in elk and bear territory after he burned the chicken we were having for dinner. David was rounding first base during our wiffleball game, the sixth of the trip, as I jogged home from third—getting pegged with a plastic ball by one of my pre-teen nephews was a more favorable outcome than outright sprinting and dissolving any sense of athleticism I still held with them. The goats roamed the field with fifteen chickens, twelve ducks, five turkeys, a few hissing geese, two ranch hands, and thirty members of my immediate family—my four siblings and I, plus our spouses, parents, and their eighteen grandkids.

I avoided a fluffy tangerine-colored rooster and almost slipped in its droppings as David rounded second; a train of five, six, eight, and nine-year-old nephews chased behind, hurling the ball as he slid into third. Some of the younger ones collapsed, screaming the phrase "not fair" more than I'd heard since teaching at an all-boys Catholic high school.

My wife, sisters, mom, and sister-in-law, the group my dad had called "the girls" the whole trip, drank wine in the Adirondack chairs, putting down their glasses to kick at pecking hens. If it were a pointillism painting, their Nike shorts and plain Target t-shirts would look more formal, but in my view, it looked more like east Texas had come to town. So I laughed when Mary Claire suggested a Bordeaux instead of my mom's boxed wine—and laughed harder when she described the Bordeaux as *quaffable.*

Everyone in their place, even the ranch hands Rex and Connor ran out to join the game, which got my dad to come to try his hand at pitching, an audience for his past-prime athleticism in cut-off scrub shorts. But as I crossed home plate, a central figure caught my eye. In front of the chair line of crossed-legged women and wine glasses, but far enough away from the pasture playing field, a light flickered through the dancing Aspen leaves onto two baby blankets. The two youngest kids, Mary Margaret and Elodie, swam in place, rolling over to giggle, spit, or eat a handful of grass. But next to them, Tommy stretched across the softer blankets, its woven cotton blunt but warm. He leaned on his elbow and crossed his legs. His mom had asked him to join the game this last time, but he was nursing an injury from a Netflix binge the day before and felt tired. He lifted a handful of something in the air.

I watched as the sun set on my family, my feet covered in chicken shit and my dad yelling at someone to toughen up, and Tommy letting a handful of Cheeto puffs fall into his tilted mouth, giggling and crunching before a brown spotted goat came staring with its rectangular pupil.

❧

A soft recorded voice brought me back to the airport tram—we were approaching our terminal. A man next to me in an oil field coat, a thick navy OSHA-looking jacket announced to his buddy it was about to rain.

"See how dark it is? Dark as shit," he said.

I looked at my kids to see if they'd hear the cuss word and think their grandfather hopped on the tram out of nowhere—they were coloring.

"About time we got some rain," the other said, his drawl as thick as the first's jacket. "We needed it."

Yeah, *we* did it, I thought.

Amoebas

I had a short and unceremonious skater phase in my adolescent years. I didn't actually skateboard, and my mom's eyes crossed when I showed her the clunky shoes, so it was more of a passing shadow of appreciation, a waning phase, but it impacts me to this day.

My friend John David lived across the street from our middle school. He was a latchkey kid, and I thought that was about the closest thing to adulthood a kid could find. There's no public transportation in Texarkana, Texas, so getting around in middle school meant walking, getting a ride with a mom, riding a bike, or staying put. A latchkey kid made his own choices—what music he listened to, what he did when he got home—and could develop his own tastes. There was no oldies sock hop hour ride home for a latchkey kid.

John David's mom, single as long as I knew her, arranged rides and lodging for the rail conductors coming through town, and this somehow landed her a spot on a voyage to the Titanic a few years later that would make the local paper. This landed JD a walk home every day of seventh grade, straight to the freedom of an empty house, a Hot Pocket or cereal bowl, and his white-walled room covered in band posters—The Offspring, Sublime, Pennywise, and Cypress Hill. Those and a Dallas Cowboy Cheerleader swimsuit calendar that his cousin was in and has signed. Cousins can be confusing.

I'd stumble through the heat to his house most days when my mom was late picking me up, probably running things up to the high school for one sister or another. I was the youngest of five, and my youngest siblings grow up adored and indulged, yet tortured. I was humored more than anything but would be the first to get left at school.

But there at John David's, in the dawn of a new millennium, I learned to play Tony Hawk's Pro Skater on his PlayStation. PlayStations, even in the infancy of gaming, had more oomph than the soft-edged Nintendo consoles my family grew up with.

The game, a zero-gravity version of skateboarding, had skateparks, architecture, hobos, and taco stands to grind on. It had it all and music.

Apart from being in Texas, Texarkana had no real DNA within the Lone Star State of mind. No country music acts of note came from East Texas. Johnny Cash and Elvis played here early in their careers, but nobody my age was pirating country western on BearShare, LimeWire or Napster. On the off chance you could get a CD from the mall, it certainly wasn't Pilotdrift, the early-2000s Christian rock group from the big-tent Baptist church in town.

My first CD was Big Willie Style by Will Smith—the musical equivalent of confusing Miracle Whip for mayonnaise.

My brother played Lynyrd Skynyrd when he drove me to school, and I believed that to be rock and roll. I also thought the lead singer must be Mr. Skynyrd. I was always bad like that with the music minutiae. Years and a Portland, Oregon address for my brother later, he'd scream, "Britt is killing it tonight!" in my ear during a concert in New Orleans.

"Who?"

"Britt!"

"Yeah, who?"

He was talking about Britt Daniel, Spoon's lead singer.

I'd surpassed JD in the act of virtual skateboarding after a couple of weeks, and I slowly took down the Jerry Rice and Cal Ripken Jr. posters in my room at home. I asked my mom if we could remove the 49ers wallpaper I'd insisted on in third grade—maybe something more tasteful like eggshell, asylum white? She didn't go for it. Besides, I was horrified of becoming a poser now, which was the first word I looked up on a new website, Urban Dictionary after John David called me one for wearing my hair like Bob Burnquist for a summer.

Burnquist was my skater of choice from Tony Hawk's game. You couldn't use the titular character, or else you, too, would grind on the path towards poser perdition. That left Burnquist, Rodney Mullen, Rune Glifberg, Eric Koston, Bucky Lasek, Geoff Rowley, Kareem Campbell, Chad Muska, Bam Margera, Steve Caballero, Elissa Steamer. Campbell, the only hint of diversity in the game for a while, we saved for when our friend Andre came over and wanted to use him. We felt good about that at the time as we drifted into pubescent racism and later misogyny.

Tony Hawk Pro Skater 2 came out on September 19th, 2000. Almost twenty-two years to the day after Space Invaders was released in Japan, and twenty-two years to the day before I'm writing this. There was a seismic leap in society and video game technology from 1978 to 2000. The same formative bounds would be established within me that year when I heard ska for the first time.

Ska is a breathless, reggae-sounding rock subgenre that I was introduced to through Sublime, Goldfinger, and Reel Big Fish, all on Tony Hawk soundtracks. It's so southern California you can taste the imported avocado. Up to that point, I was living a lie, and as far as I was concerned, a light had been shown on it. I liked this music, and it was mine. It was, in many ways, my first act of contrarianism outside of hating Pokémon.

Ska was the gateway to punk and alternative music. It was inviting and easy listening compared to Dead Kennedys, whose logo looked like it was picked off the Third Reich's propaganda scrapbooking room floor.

The soundtrack also carried acts like Fu Manchu, who was anything but ska. Softcore punk like The Ramones, Bodyjar, and Fenix, TX gave way to thicker, saltier punk like CKY, AFI, Suicidal Tendencies, The Mad Capsule Markets, Guttermouth, Pennywise, The Cult, and my favorite, The Adolescents. Then the harder, faster metal groups mixed into each session by passing the video game controller back and forth, getting another turn and seeping in the music. Motörhead, Black Sabbath, Anthrax, and System of a Down—stuff our older brothers were scared of.

Other kids eventually joined us, as did other games. Marketed as more *extreme*, which was the nom de plume for violent, blood-spewing good times, Dave Mirra's Freestyle BMX came out with a similar mix of bone-cracking and alternative genres. The culture was changing—Jackass was on the rise. (John David and our friend Cody would make a PG-version of Jackass they titled Sausage—one of the stunts involved asking someone's mom at Friday football game's concession stand for a Frito pie, then freaking out when it wasn't an actual pie.)

We sectioned off into clusters of groupies. Cody and John David liked Sublime and CKY. I was into Pennywise, which penned the song I walked to plate to in baseball our senior year. We fell in with Megadeth fans in school for a while, and two friends, Matt and Kyle, started a punk band. Patrick stayed with Megadeth. Hunter and Matthew liked Dead Kennedys. Our love and knowledge for the groups were pure and genuine, even if I didn't know the lead singers' names.

Then the sandbox was opened to the hip-hop acts in later iterations of the game. The smooth ones like De La Soul, Tribe Called Quest, Gang Starr, and Del The Phunky Homosapien, and the formidably harsh, almost stifling, almost punk, Public Enemy, NWA, Ozomatli, and Exhibit, all of whom I'd squeeze out every bit of street cred I could when teaching at a majority-black school years later. Up to that point, I'd assumed "Gettin' Jiggy Wit It" and whatever song our gym coach turned up while we threw dodgeballs at each other ("You Dropped a Bomb On Me" by The Gap Band) was an urban afternoon. Beau liked Three 6 Mafia, who later appeared on Jackass, and Edward followed NWA, DJ Yella in particular, before he and a few friends started a rap group—The Velociraptor Clique.

A Pitchfork review of De La Soul once said they gave us a glimpse into their coming-of-age, and "let us listen to the sound of three (well, four) Americans working out how to hear each other and move forward together in a cruel world," and they and Tony Hawk Pro Skater 2 did just that for me and my East Texas friends looking for a sanctuary from the crusading melodrama of Christian rock. And it all started with ska. Ska was the blueprint for cool until your first joint.

Good art makes you understand yourself, and pot helps a sophomore in high school understand art and Primus.

We went to John David's pristinely grunge room again a year or two into high school. In our second year on the JV baseball team and in no rush to get to practice, he pulled a hobbled twig out of a drawer in his room. Roxy and Maxine, two small Scottish Terriers—dogs my dad called yippy dogs—scratched at the door, barking and gnawing at the lip of the door.

We smoked it and played Tony Hawk. They'd added more blood to the game since the first years, and we crashed enough our skaters should've hemorrhaged before the second song.

But that first time you can hear a song never leaves you, and neither does the first time you can understand it. We listened and didn't have much to say. We thought we were immortal and had time to talk later. I stared into the sun of a Sublime logo on JD's wall.

I stared into the sequin eyes of Superman on a blue jean jacket a few weeks later—the hero's face swaying, lunging forward and backward as John David tried to keep his balance in front of the high school principal at a school dance.

"You... don't like my jack-et?" he said, showing off the bright pattern, his head bobbing like a cork and his eyes blinking too much. The seniors, the ones he was hanging out with now, got him drunk and high before the dance, and that effectively ended my seeing John David for a while. I got an older girlfriend who introduced me to bagged wine and Citizen Cope. Then I failed AP English, and the older girlfriend was gone, and I sat despaired, briefly considering changing the red and gold 49er wallpaper in my room again.

By the time JD and I emerged from parent-induced hiding, Pennywise, and The Offspring were gone. Everyone was making quarterly pilgrimages to an area outside Houston, Texas, for field shows of the Dave Matthews Band, or "Dave," as my older girlfriend had called them. I would eventually marry a girl that referred to Dave Matthews Band as "DMB" and, in her high school years, loved bands like Incubus. She got onto me for adding a Yo La Tengo track to our first baby's bottle-time playlist, asking if I was depressed or just wanted the baby to be. Sorry it wasn't Taking Back fucking Sunday.

Things were ending or changing all around me, and for once, I seemed to be right. Graduation was coming up, and our dreams of attending the Warped Tour shifted as I took up with Modest Mouse, The Hives, People Under the Stairs, and the Beastie Boys—music for dropping into a half-pipe and using another.

These rap groups mixed with the guitars, horns, and drumbeats of punk to form an unprecedented cohesion of sound. There might've been no better place to enter the psyche of a teenager in the early-2000s than a video game. It took a while for us to realize that no matter the genre—Black Sabbath, KRS-One, Geto Boys, Sublime, Gang Starr, etc. –these guys weren't talking about cars, women, or taking down the man, they were all discussing the paranoia and anxiety of growing up and, more importantly for a teenage boy, failing.

How a human deals with the notion of failure and with having failed. A person, and again, particularly a teenage boy and maybe more so one from nowhere, is a fallible entity, and learning to accept this is a key to life. John David skated, but most of us didn't have an offscreen board to get back up on, so life would have to do.

We graduated high school and went our separate state-funded ways. Me to LSU, John David and a slew to the University of Arkansas, and a more select few to University of Texas. A couple of real sinister-types went on to Texas A&M.

In college, a friend told me I reminded her of Isaac Brock.

"Who?"

"The lead singer of this band I like. Modest Mouse," she'd said.

I made sure to compensate by using a newish website, Wikipedia, to learn the rest of the band and prove I was hip. The background of Wikipedia is violently stark, giving off the perfect apathetic early 2000s beginner's web design free tutorial like they couldn't be bothered to add more pictures. No pomp or circumstance, just unfiltered knowledge. Securely not posing.

Like the posters on John David's walls.

Now in my thirties, I donate to Wikipedia monthly. Directly from my children's mouths into my one true source of information.

I miss learning about punk rock and hip hop in John David's white-walled room, acting like we could play guitar, and hearing Adolescents and Del the Funky Homosapien for the first time. Walking across the busy street next to the middle school. Sitting on his trampoline. Him calling me a poser. Knowing latchkey kids beyond my own.

Family Focused

They never wheel in the big TVs anymore. The creaking wheels of the faded blue carts, the slight teacher wrestling it around desks and chairs like a riot cop.

I saw one during the pandemic while working in a nursing home in south Louisiana—we'd roll one into the dining room for movie night—at 1 PM each day. It was always the same movie: *Red River* starring John Wayne and Montgomery Clift about a cattle drive. We'd draw the blinds and lower the lamps, making sure to hover just above industry lighting standards so they could see the big bubble of a T.V. but also locate their walkers. The only one that realized it was the same movie was a blind man that would scream, "Oh, no, shit!" each time the orchestral boom of the rolling title credits fizzled out of the retrofitted speakers I'd rigged on the side. Then he'd scream about where all his Medicaid money had "run oft to" if we could only afford one DVD.

We weren't as blunt each time Senora Balhoff pulled in the blue cart, TV strapped down like a sick prisoner, as a sixth grader lowered the lights.

"Gracias, Senora Balhoff," we'd say, nodding our heads closer to the desks. The school had more than one DVD, but only one in Spanish: *Gone in 60 Seconds*, which Josh Brine, an eighth grader that already worked at the movie theater, once called "Made in 60 Seconds," which made Will Thomas flip a desk. Will was a little high-strung but, like my dad, never caught wanting for passion when it came to Nic Cage.

Gone in 60 Seconds is a PG-13 movie that's actual tagline is something about "boosting cars" and having fun doing it. There's a line that a late-90s blond Angelina Jolie delivers to Nic Cage about what's more exciting, "having sex or boosting cars?" My mom finally got to the bottom of the movie when I insisted on "boosting" a buggy from the grocery store instead of grabbing her one as she'd asked.

My friend Hunter had to sit in the hallway each time the TV rolled in—his mom found out about *Gone in 60 Seconds* years before.

Hunter's mom checked any potential film experience with a Christian review website – Family Focused. Cross-referenced with the King James Bible, the page scored every movie by how many non-biblical curse words, sexual or suggestive glances, or deaths appeared on screen. It used a simple system of red, green, and yellow lights for each category, then a short description.

> Fratricide: *green light.*
>
> Flooding an entire planet to teach someone a lesson: *yellow light.*

Just a few months before, we tried to go see *Jurassic Park III* at Cinemark XII. We found Hunter's mom and our ride, studying Family Focused and relaying the bad news: too many deaths, too much cussin', and seventy-five too many dinosaurs for the bible to make sense.

> Velociraptor cracking a man's neck then devouring his head: *red, deep red, light.*

We were as disappointed that day as Hunter was embarrassed each class Senora Balhoff pushed in the TV cart. He'd slump his shoulders, let out a knowing groan, then grab his bag and head toward the door.

> Boostin' cars and having sex: *red light.*

I sometimes wonder what Family Focused would say about *Frozen.* I can see "Let it Go," in particular, giving them some grief. Or a recent Pixar movie that says "stupid" in Italian a couple of times, which I contend is solely responsible for my three-year-old's Euro-centric cursing tangents and not *The Sopranos.*

Through the first month of the school year, we'd experienced the thrills of Cage and Jolie's escapades four times, and, if memory serves, I was catching onto my Spanish pretty well. "¡Acabo de robar cincuenta autos en una noche!" Which roughly translates to, "I just stole fifty cars in one night!"

One morning, Senora Balhoff nudged the corner of the cart around the classroom door's frame, teasing us with another viewing. She was such a small woman. One shoulder jammed into a long leg of the cart as her foot propelled her body, pushing off the white cinderblock classroom's walls. Her black hair hung down to her perpetually floral dresses, which she'd shake and flattened once one of the eighth graders finally hopped up to help her.

I'd been scared of her since she caught me cheating off my friend Tommy the year before. Tommy's mom, like Senora Balhoff, was born in Argentina but lucky enough to marry a pasty man from east Texas, likely of German or British descent. The vocabulary word I stole from Tommy was "dinosaurio."

Will Thomas jumped to move the TV today, and Hunter begrudgingly grabbed his bag when Senora Balhoff stopped him with a raised eyebrow glance and soft palm raised over her head.

"Clase," she said, stopping to catch her breath. "Class! I have an announcement. Cazador, please sit down. I think you can stay."

Hunter turned back to our group with a surprised but confident look.

"We are not watching *60 Segundos* today. But," she paused to let us calm down, and for Hunter groaning, I think he thought he'd get to see Cage this time.

"I am going to turn the TV on under one condition. You stay calm. If you need to go to the office, you can, but you should stay calm." A blanket of confusion draped from the humming fluorescent lights, and she fiddled with some long green cords.

It made its way to our corner that we might be watching the *Romeo and Juliet* cassette tape from Mrs. Copeland's English class, the one where Juliet might as well be nude, but we'd never know since Mrs. Copeland skipped over each potentially passionate scene.

When they got it hooked up, the static rolled over the screen, and Senora Balhoff scooted to the side, punching down the volume button. The screen began to focus and skip, then roll like eyes into the back of its head. The picture was rotating around the toilet roll of the TV, then wobbling to a stop somewhere in the middle, and all I could see was smoke.

It was the first time I understood the phrase "clouds of smoke." Then they showed the replay, like a sports highlight, a plane hurling into a tall building. It was the first time I understood how fast planes are traveling.

Some of the girls started spontaneously chirping, sounds of distress. Senora Balhoff was sitting back at her desk, her head resting in her hands, black hair shooting between her short fingers like dark waterfalls as her shoulders bounced. Parents started showing up at the school to pick up kids in case a plane was diverted to a small east Texas middle school.

The intercom prickled overhead, and someone in the front office coughed as they tended to do before making an announcement.

"Mrs. Bal-Hoff?"

"¿Si?"

"Britney's mom is here to pick her up. Send her to the front office, please."

"Hunter is needed to the office, too. His mom is here to pick him up."

9/11: *red light.*

East Texas remains segregated from significance on the cultural landscape (outside of a former resident's run for president and my friend Joseph's sister making it into the background of a *Game of Thrones* episode), but the geographical anonymity which can sometimes border on all out isolation cocoons the area from the true vehicles of disaster. It's too far south for blizzards, too many trees for significant tornados, and the only thing you might want to bomb is the dowdy old water tower with the "Twice as Nice" slogan. When the last gasps of Hurricane Katrina reached us in 2005, we played the greatest game of storm soccer there ever was. We went slipping through the rain and mud as the ball spontaneously lifted and swirled this way or that, crashing back into someone's ribs or the goal. The same wind that broke buildings and tore through lives a few hundred miles south provided me with an indelible memory. One that I hope to remember when they wheel in the TV for me and play *Red River* or, again with great hope, *Gone in 60 Seconds.*

We had recess on 9-11.

Rolling out of the classroom doors, I found a few friends, one of which was on his way to the principal's office for saying he thought this type of thing happened in other countries all the time, so why should he care? The rest of us filed slowly to the playground in the back of the school, the pace quickening when the herd rounded the last corner.

My wife and kids evacuated to east Texas during Hurricane Ida in 2021 while I stayed behind to show my blind friend *Red River.* My wife, Melissa, sent me videos of the kids, which flooded my phone at once when I made the daily pilgrimage to the interstate, where my phone's carrier provided a sliver of service. They were running across our family cabin's lawn at the lake, Henry barely able to waddle after Flannery's three-year-old screeches of excitement. "You can do it, Henry!" some adults said in the background.

Then I saw the blink of a firefly just above the driveway, the sky darkening but not yet asleep, as my daughter would say. I filled entire mason jars with them when I was a kid, but with the humidity in south Louisiana, I realized this was the first time they were seeing fireflies or "lightnin' bugs" my mom made them repeat in an East Texas accent. Flannery broke into a run, her arms bent at the elbow, a determined and optimistic look in her eye that faded as the blinking light when out before she could reach it. Henry's method was more cupped hands and blind faith, grasping at air and opening his mouth.

It was getting late in the summer, and the cicadas were buzzing in the trees enough that my phone vibrated if I turned the volume up. A couple more blinked across my phone screen as Henry tumbled forward in his attempt to turn (He won't be an NFL receiver).

And then she caught one, running it over to Melissa and squealing as hints of light pierced her little fingers. She looked through a little hole between her thumb and pointer, then screamed as the bug flew, determined and frightened, into her eye.

After some exaggerated tears and light petting from her mom, I watched as Flannery strode confidently, happily, back into the meadow and knew that she'd never forget her first hurricane evacuation.

To have children is to have complete responsibility for another human being and to love and bond in the deepest way. There's no substitute—not even old folks in crisis.

ꝏ

We were eventually called back into the school, but now the local Baptist youth minister roamed the halls asking if we needed someone to talk to. Mrs. Snyder, our seventh-grade social studies teacher, told him to get lost and slumped behind her desk. Her brownish gray hair perched on her head like an hourglass, she looked frazzled as she announced that those of us left could have a free period. Those of us left were either working moms' kids or kids with at least four siblings whose parents weren't going to let a terrorist attack interrupt a previously scheduled day of peace.

My friend John David, his mom stuck at work coordinating rides for the train conductors rolling through town, performed tricks with a miniature skateboard up and down the wooden desk, his fingers grinding it across the metal bar that attached the seat to the desktop (I'd watch a kid in Houston break that metal bar off years later during my first teaching job. She broke it off and beat another kid across the head and neck with it, cutting her and ruining a white button-up I'd worn that day. This is where my first and last bit of street cred came from—I broke up a fight then had an extra button-down in my car. The kids loved what would be the coolest and whitest moment of my life).

They played "I'm Proud to be an American" on the intercom, which sent Mrs. Synder into a fit of tears. Some kids stood to salute the flag. Mrs. Synder took down the Texas flag that usually hung near or above the

American one, not out of protest but probably because of all places you can get away with it—it's probably east Texas.

Disaster rages through our world, mine less so now that I'm away from the nursing home business. "It's getting worse out there," I caught myself saying one week this pandemic, like I was on the frontier, flanked by a family that needs water before succumbing to dysentery.

I don't know if it's getting worse, but I can only hope when the next disaster comes, my kids get to watch it on TV.

Bonjour Y'all

We watched *Con Air* in spurts, passing from the kitchen to the den to the beer fridge in the back-laundry room, while my dad laid back in his fold-out leather chair, drinking his iced milk. It was as close to a Christmas tradition we'd had in the last decade. Dad would call us in, waving his hand around like a third-base coach, giddy as each felon went through the roll call—Cyrus the Virus was his favorite.

We used to take family trips around Christmas, usually skiing or to Shreveport, but those ended after an ill-fated Carnival Cruise in 2003. My dad's asthma kicked up during a SCUBA diving tour and almost killed him, I was served a twenty-year-old Sprite in a glass bottle while deep sea fishing and spent the rest of the excursion puking over the side while a goth kid reeled in tuna and flounder the size of my torso—high-fiving his grandfather the whole way through right in my green face. I also got stung by a wasp, on my eyelid, somewhere out in the Gulf of Mexico, while wandering the lido deck looking for spare change to turn play a video arcade game in the "Teen Lounge." I was then confined to my swashing, swaying room the rest of the trip where the only movies that would come on were *The Stepford Wives*, Hillary Duff's *Raise Your Voice,* and, ironically, *The Terminal* with Tom Hanks, where he can't leave an airport terminal—I sympathized with Tom. Our last trip skiing saw a ten-year-old me get lost in the hustle and bustle of Crusted Butte, Colorado. Separated from my family in a blizzard, a large bald man with a boa constrictor around his shoulders helped me find my way to the ski lodge and nervous ski instructor that lost me in the snowbank. In high school we would ride around town and tackle inflatable decorations until my car was pointed out in the "Cheers and Jeers" section of the local paper, ending our short streak of yuletide hijinks. I took to watching the movie with my dad in full when my college Christmas tradition—all my friends in town for the holidays meeting at Fat Jack's, a local bar—went up in smoke after I got too drunk and broke a glass bottle on the shuffleboard table and wrote my friend's cell-phone number in blood on the center. I was politely asked not to return, and even though I'm not sure how enforceable the ban could possibly be, the fear of being turned away by whatever substitute teacher or middle school coach of mine they had watching the door that night was too much.

After the *Con Air* ended in 2018—Cyrus the Virus finally brought to justice by a scrap metal compactor and Nic Cage reunited with his hummingbird—my mom invited us into the sprawling living room—one of the only carpeted rooms in the house, it saw little use outside our Christmas mornings or graduation party dinners. The fireplace was a golden red, roaring through the metal grate and causing me to sweat through my t-shirt and shorts when I huddled onto one of the plush couches. Above the flames hung three scarlet ibis paintings my mom bought from a store in Baton Rouge when I was in college. I got her a door sign that read *Bonjour Y'all* the year before from this little antique market. My parents being from Louisiana but raising kids in Texas, they thought the sign a trademark. My mom had to go by the market each time she was in town to see if they had any other witty sayings or noteworthy pieces. The ibises lurk behind hanging gobs of Spanish moss, their feet disappearing in the murky swamp water as they look down on my family in the bursting light of the fire.

It was our first time together since my brother-in-law pulled a gun on my other brother-in-law during my rehearsal dinner. They've both subsequently assured me that the event never happened, but much like Santa Claus or the Texas Rangers' World Series odds, I still choose to believe. This would be the last Christmas before one of my four siblings needed to find a hotel for either more room or more headspace rather than squeeze everyone in the six-bedroom home we'd grown up in.

ꝏ

My dad sat in the one armchair in the room and pulled up his scrub pants to show us what he'd gotten from my mom—compression socks and Sketcher ShapeUp walking shoes, the kind with the round, half-moon bottoms that rocked like a porch chair, which he demonstrated—then he slunk back in the chair and swirled his ice milk again, directing attention to my mom.

"So, you know," she said, fidgeting with a row of presents stacked in columns of three, each with a Charlie Brown wrapping paper. "It's been a while since we've seen each other, all of us together like this."

I could tell she was choking back either genuine remorse or frustration with us all.

"Like this, as a group. Together."

"We get it, mom, come on," my sister Leigh said, sipping a glass of wine. Her six kids were down to bed and Leigh didn't play around with her free time.

"Okay, okay… we haven't had Christmas all of us together in a long time and who knows the next time we will, so I thought it would be fun to make this one more memorable." She was straightening the top boxes, perking up their bows as she spoke. "So, we're going to play a game. White Elephant, Dirty Santa—the game you pick a present, open it, then someone can steal it, or you're stuck with it. And the rule, the *rule*, is that something can only be stolen twice. Twice, and then it's that person's gift. I have enough gifts for everyone to go home with two gifts, so each couple will have four to bring home."

"You did all this? You picked out all of the gifts?" my brother David asked.

"I did. And your dad." My dad raised his Houston Astros commemorative stadium cup in the air.

There were some glazed nods of approval, both in apprehension and acceptance that this was going to happen because she'd set it up and we needed to act happy about it no matter how many cat mugs or scarlet ibis coasters were hiding in these boxes.

"Well, thank you, mom," David said. "Let's pick the order? Jac likes winning these games." Jacqueline, David's wife and one of the top ophthalmology residents in the country, did like winning at things like this, but she hated saying it. David did, too, but there aren't very many aggressive pediatricians.

As for Melissa and me, we would take the road seldom traveled in this group—the middle road, slightly left of center but never any potholes or friction between us and a sibling or in-law. I once yelled at my youngest sister Mary Claire's boyfriend, and Melissa did that head bob maneuver from those Real Housewife shows where you know she's ready to roll if need be, so I was quasi-aware she had my back in White Elephant. But she'd also made the mistake of revealing her high school yearbook superlative was "Best Hair," so each sibling Secret Santa came with a new hair product in case she hadn't moved on from high school.

Mary Claire was up first. She jokingly juggled a few small boxes before picking a sensible medium-sized package in deep red wrapping paper, Charlie Brown sitting on the side with a Santa hat. After loosening the tape and unfolding the wrapping paper, careful to save it for next year, she let out a laugh.

"Oh, wow. A… a wine glass that is big enough to hold an entire bottle of wine!"

She flashed the box at the crowd, all of us laughing as Leigh sarcastically clamored for it, simultaneously asking her husband James for a top off on her own glass.

"Someone's going to steal that for sure," my mom said.

"Oh, let's hope so," Mary Claire said, setting it down on the rug next to her feet. "I'm not totally sure I can even fly with something like that."

"I can mail it to you," my mom said.

"No, that's okay," Mary Claire said.

Next was Melissa. Of the stacks of boxes, there was one that teetered on the edge of collapse, its base box just a hair bigger than the rest. I instructed Mel to go straight for the biggest box. "The best gift is never in the biggest box," she whispered.

"Who—cares?" I said back. "My mom isn't trying to trick us. That's the biggest box because that's the biggest gift. Get it."

"Okay," Melissa shouted over the crowd, "here we go. Nice wrapping paper… well wrapped… it's big and that's what Casey said he wanted… so… I'm opening it… and… um." Her face looked like there was a live muskrat in the bottom of the box, not so much compassion as confusion. Her hand reached in and out came an endless stream of plush burgundy cloth with gold tassels haphazardly coming into view. She stood up and pulled with her knees, grabbing more and more like a magician's assistant. When she finished, she was like a little bug sitting inside a blossoming rose.

"What is it?" Melissa asked.

The room was quiet as I reached out to touch it. It was musty on my finger, damp but soft at the same time, like a dog that just dried off after a swim. Or what I imagine a sweating camel feels like. But this was cold, too.

"Mom, what is this?" my oldest sibling Katie asked, looking over my shoulder. "Is that…"

"I thought some of you would recognize it, but I guess not." My mom looked disappointed. "That's Aunt Dee Dee's formal duvet."

"Aunt Dee Dee?" Melissa said, holding it up like she was now caught in a spider web. "How am I supposed to know who that is?"

Aunt Dee Dee was my mom's great aunt who had a daughter named Claire that ran into a pot of boiling gumbo one day and was scalded so bad that she passed away. My mom decided to name her last daughter after the girl—and the Virgin Mary—so Mary Claire now sat just a few feet away from what was presumably her namesake's conception garment, if it was a formal night. Years later, Mary Claire would name her daughter Elodie, and when I asked where she found that name, she said: "Well, it's Aunt Dee Dee's real name, of course." Of course, I said.

Katie, the only one with any memory of Aunt Dee Dee, looked dejected as the rest of us scrambled to develop a strategy.

"Mom," Katie said. "Why put something like that in this game? You know I'd want that."

"Then steal it," my mom said, shrugging but with a bit of mischief in her voice. "It hasn't been stolen… yet!"

"Is this real?" my brother-in-law Steve, Katie's husband, asked. Steve was a trauma surgeon and had little time for emotional currency in moments like this.

"Yes," my mom said, her chin rising to the ceiling.

"And I got a wine glass?" Mary Claire said, kicking the box by her feet.

"Okay, focus, Katie," Steve said. "We don't need the comforter. Or we can wait. Melissa doesn't want that. It's gross. Nobody wants that. Get gifts out in the open now, then we can steal later. That comforter isn't the best item, surely. Focus!"

David was quiet. James was coming back in with a glass of wine for Leigh. James, a Harvard Law man, also enjoyed winning games like this but the years of six children (seven today) had softened him. But Leigh was ready, passing on the wine refill.

Mary Claire's husband Brent took a knee near Mary Claire and developed a communication system. Brent was up next.

"Steal the wine glass, please," Mary Claire said. "Then I'll be able to get something else."

Brent tapped Mary Claire on the shoulder, biting his lip. "No… no, I don't think I will." And strode toward the phalanx of wrapping.

He opened part of my mom's porcelain nativity set she displayed every year. Mary Claire seemed pleased; Katie whimpered behind.

Someone asked if they were dying, and my dad cracked up and said, "hopefully."

I went next, tearing into the Linus and Lucy paper, revealing the colorful spines of the vintage ChildCraft "How and Why" 1980 Fifteen Volume Encyclopedia set—the same set my dad would sit me on his lap and read at night. I learned about animals and folk tales and volcanoes and space. Cinderella and the three little pigs—the Brothers Grimm or someone old's version, not Walt Disney.

"What the fuck," I said under my breath, still not wanting my mom to know I knew that word. "No, no, no."

"Yeahhh, I'll take that." David was up and striding across the room. In an instant he snatched the box of books and plopped them next to Jacqueline, who was up after David.

"Wait—isn't it my turn?" I said.

"Yes, but you can't steal back what's already been stolen this round," David said.

"Okay, but if I steal the comforter then Melissa can, hypothetically, steal the books, right? Right?"

"I say only one steal per round," David said, in a tone only an older brother can muster.

"Mom?" I said, sweeping the room to find her organizing the remaining boxes. "Mom, this is crazy."

"Oh, no it's not. Only one steal per round or we'd be here all night. If you want the duvet, get the duvet. It's not a comforter like you get at Bed Bath and Beyond."

"You can have the wine glass."

I walked to the pile and pulled another box. My mom's old spoon collection. There were over thirty spoons, some older than me, some older than my mom, some from a hot dog vender in the French Quarter.

Jacqueline, at the direction of her husband which I found unbecoming of a top ophthalmology fellow, stole the ChildCraft "How and Why" 1980 Fifteen Volume Encyclopedia set, locking it into their family, which currently lived in London so they wouldn't even fly back with them anyway.

Katie opened an American Girl doll they'd collected as kids. "I forgot about these," she said, brushing Samantha or Amanda or Lydia's hair to the side, a stream of tears now visible across the room.

James grabbed a long, slender box. My dad sat up when James jingled it next to his ear.

"Oh, James, you'll like that one," he said. "That's one of mine. And with all those kids, you'll probably use it, too. Maybe on yourself."

James slid his hand in the box and his face went stiff as he slowly pulled out my grandfather's double barrel shotgun—the one he'd given my dad for his medical school graduation, that my dad figured out was stolen in Mexico after reconfiguring the scratched-out serial numbers.

"All right!" James shouted.

"Dad!" David yelled. Steve stomped his foot in excitement, he was up next.

"I'm stealing Dennis's gun!"

"No!" shouted James.

"Dad!" David continued. "We went hunting together with that gun. Is this like an interactive will? If you're dying just give it to me."

My dad was giggling, the type of uncontrolled cackle I only see him do during a funny beer commercial. He shrugged his shoulders and said, "Your mom needed stuff for the game!"

There was a set of four gold-embroidered mint julep cups in desperate need of polish.

"Those were my dad's," my mom said. "Look, initials are engraved and a little quote about being a pediatrician. They're from before World War II. They might've been his dad's."

"Okay, what the hell, mom," David said. "I should've just been given those cups. This is absurd."

James said he'd give them to David, but my mom put a stop to any unsanctioned trading in the middle of the game. She reminded us to stick to the rules, and everyone would end up with something special, she was sure of it.

Next was a Sharper Image Epsom salt two-in-one foot bath and massager.

"That's one of mine, too!" my dad shouted, pounding his knee as Leigh shook her head. "Hell, I'd steal that for real."

"Are there other gag gifts?" Leigh asked.

My mom looked shocked. "*Gag* gift, Leigh? It's probably more expensive than anything opened so far except the gun. And the duvet, which is *nice*."

It was Mary Claire's turn again.

"I'm not going first *again* and getting *another* wine glass. This is still available, by the way." Mary Claire fumbled to find the box.

Sensing an opportunity to soothe a situation and take the middle road, I nudged Mel.

"Melissa will go. And we can work backwards from her, with MC at the end. How's that?"

"Well, that's not exactly fair to Melissa," my mom said.

"That's okay, Mrs. Malise," Mel said, standing to study the gifts. "I won't listen to Casey this time, and I should be good." In the hierarchy of in-laws, Mel scored points with my parents early, and she scored often.

She grabbed a box with a sleek bow bobbing on top and slid it off, and after folding back a corner of wrapping, she giggled. "Oh, this is great!"

She went to unwrapping, peeling off the paper to reveal a piece of my mom's snow village collection, a snow and wreath covered Starbucks Coffee house.

Then there was a box of letters my dad's mom wrote to my grandfather when he was serving in World War II. "The history teacher gets the history heirloom," my dad said excitedly as Brent shuffled through the letters. Brent was a Spanish teacher. Mary Claire's old boyfriend, the one I'd yelled at, was the history teacher.

My turn, I was ready to take the gun and force a backroom trade for the encyclopedia set. I knew David couldn't resist it. But the draw of the box pile called. And I picked a small box, one that rattled like a dog collar.

Inside was my great grandmother's rosary, silver browning and dull. But the beads shone bright, clearly rubbed violently in deep prayer. Katie whimpered again.

David stole the mint julep cups.

Then there was a set of diamond earrings that Katie promptly stole, before Leigh stole them a second time, leading Katie to take the rosary, me opening an old gumbo pot which made Aunt Dee Dee's duvet twitch. Jacqueline ended up with a watch. Katie opened and cried over our Mamere's—my mom's mom—handwritten recipe book. Katie owned a workout studio, so I doubt she ever makes much etouffee or blackberry pie, but who knows.

James ended up with a set of Christmas-themed whiskey glasses that he promptly filled with shots for everyone in the room. Steve got some very old baseball cards, and Mary Claire settled on a gift—a photo album from our family vacations to Wyoming. All of us in white Old Navy shirts, riding horseback through mountain ranges.

My mom remembered one last gift she forgot to include. "Just a fun one," she said, signifying it was what we thought as a gag gift. It was a Garfield Christmas tree ornament.

"Mom, I would have thrown a real fit if I'd picked that one."

"Well, you didn't. So hush. Everyone's happy, right? Was this fun?"

We agreed. Some of us quickly inventoried our bounty, Steve taking the shotgun outside with my dad. Katie was on the blue couch in the corner, wiping her eyes.

Again, an opportunity.

We gave her the formal duvet. It was the least we could do.

"I think we'll do this again. White Elephant was a little more fun than Secret Santa or whatever y'all did before," she said, then began reading from her phone. "White Elephant, the phrase, is said to come from the historic practice of the King of Siam giving rare albino elephants to courtiers who had displeased him, so that they might be ruined by the animals' upkeep costs. It signifies an extravagant, impractical gift that cannot be easily disposed of."

A family, I thought.

Wild Pack of Family Dogs

He was most known for his sensitivity and demonstrations against political conversations. When my siblings would come home for the holidays, all either married or dating by this time, I'd retreat to our living room before the Obama vs. McCain discussions kicked up. There I'd find our cocker spaniel Bandit, red rocket out, scooting across the grainy Persian rug with his back legs kicked out, front paws propelling him forward, satisfying the oldest itches in history—often simultaneously. *This guy knows what's important*, I'd think. And that summed up my political leaning until I had children.

Growing up, we had a slew of mutts and pure breeds. Black and white, beagles and Labradors, one that the seller said was half coyote, the dogs roamed our neighborhood on the outskirts of town, sometimes escaping across a bridge at the back of the yard and running after squirrels for days. Many an afternoon and vocal muscle exhausted screaming their names into the bottoms of the trees from our back porch. If they didn't come within a few minutes of calling, "I guess they just don't wanna eat," my dad would conclude.

When I got a dog of my own in college, I half-based his name on how it sounded at a high, panicked pitch, envisioning him sprinting into a crowd of geese, trailing a squirrel, or humping a leg. The other half based on my favorite Beastie Boys' song.

Most of them had an old baseball player's name. We had Kirby, a black lab named after a black baseball player, until my mom ran him over with the family's black suburban one afternoon on our newly paved street. My brother David hunched over Kirby's body, he'd screamed for my mom to stop the car, but she was late taking my sisters to ballet on the Arkansas side of town and had to hurry. My brother was training Kirby on duck hunting commands when he took off after the yellow boot on one of the Goodyear tires. My dad decided it was a good time to invest in professional trainers for the hunting dogs.

The city would repave our road: three houses on nine acres across the street from a car dealership owner with horses, cows, and a prop-plane runway. The three houses on our side shared a small artificial pond with a scrubby island growing in the middle. The island was suitable for campouts when the weather cooled down, but it was even better for smoking weed when I grew up.

Kirby was just one of many poorly trained hunting dogs. Spud was the eldest, or I should say Spud lasted the longest. He was named after a baseball player at a local high school. A white kid this time.

Chipper was a minuscule mutt, shabby and small as the island in the lake. He was named after Chipper Jones, the Atlanta Braves' third baseman in the 90s. My mom always told us about Chipper Jones getting divorced and how his wife had to leave Atlanta because he was so popular. I didn't know it then, but that would be a lifelong ambition—become so popular that your ex-wife has to leave town after you dump her once you're famous. Our Chipper died when the UPS truck clipped him one morning while my dad and I were playing catch in the front yard. He limped into my arms and went cold.

Chipper went into the sideyard cemetery next to Ranger, a springer spaniel named after the professional baseball team from Dallas, and was joined shortly by Maggie, a loud-mouthed beagle named after a Van Morrison song. I can't remember how Maggie died, but it had to be from some form of blunt-force trauma—the easiest way to go out, I've learned from life and Dateline. Gus was over there, too. Gus was either named after a baseball player or the chubby mouse from *Cinderella*—either way, decent yellin' name.

The cemetery rested along our half-circle driveway, next to a line of pine trees. During high school, my mom taught our foreign exchange student how to garden with a large wooden planter box she left in front of the crooked wooden crosses sticking up, jagged and catawampus from the floor of pine needles, their wooden planks wobbling on the nails like a line of parading Rockettes.

We tried a string of Louisiana-centric names for a year or two when Parvo swept through the property. Gumbo, Roux, and Tchoupitoulas, who we called Chop, all died within a year. A distinct smell hung in our garage for years, something spoiled but sweet that I associated with the time Gumbo, a furry ball no taller than my knee, puked all over the smooth polished concrete next to my dad's first sportscar—a white 1965 Corvette Stingray. Splat, right on the front wheel. We got rid of the car soon after the dog.

Things took a literary and industrial turn a few years later when we poured a concrete slab in the back yard with two chain-link enclosures on either side and stuck a white lab puppy in there named Scout.

Scout was a good dog and mother to my college dog—Paul Revere (named after the Beastie Boys song, not the historical figure).

As for the mutts, the most consequential came one Christmas morning when my middle sister Leigh—who was going through a frizzy-haired, braces, and acne phase—got a monochromatic, long-haired mutt of doubtful pedigree that she named Bandit for absolutely no reason.

People used to say we were all so smart that even our dogs were smart. Not Bandit. He was a savant.

Walking around half the time with his slimy little red rocket unsheathed, Bandit was always on edge, as anyone with their penis consistently out might be. He barked at the wind, causing my dad to run across the house with a pillow in one hand and a beer in the other, swinging one of them wildly as Bandit scampered up the stairs. He once impregnated the car dealer's German shepherd, a police K9 academy dropout dog that scared the hell out of everyone who saw her. "These are y'all's, and keep this shit outta our yard," he said one day, dropping off a box of black and white mutts. Bandit watched with a cold understanding as we sold each one away, always the consummate capitalist.

The neighborhood was home to a roaming gang of dogs led by our neighbor, an ear, nose, and throat surgeon. Dr. Michaels would walk around the neighborhood every day after his wife and kids left him, always with a fresh pack of deli meat from the Albertson's counter. By the time he got a mile or two down the road, he had a train of ten dogs sniffing his heels, and after the first couple of weeks of this daily routine, the dogs wised up and stayed in his front yard, keeping watch over his comings and goings. Our kennels were full with Scout and Spud, so Bandit walked the neighborhood freely, impregnating and gorging on bologna.

We didn't see him for about a year when he lived with the pack at Dr. Michaels' house but we'd catch stolen glimpses out the kitchen window as they took off on their daily pilgrimage around the neighborhood. Now and then, I'd get fussed at enough to take the trashcans up our long hill of a driveway and find Bandit escaping the heat in the drainage ditch's buildup near our mailbox. I'd call for him, but he'd saunter out of the water and run, his long, ungroomed mop of a body swishing down the road back to his new house.

Some nights you'd be on the porch and look up to feel eyes on you from somewhere in the dark patches of our yard. Our house didn't emit much light until we had spotlights put in the pine trees that survived a freeze in 2004, then their long shadows stretched to the prop plane runway across the street. But in the dark, only crickets and cicadas blurring the calm of the moment, you'd slowly stand to make your way across the brick floor until the rush of dogs caught your ear, and you seized as the onslaught of barking from the pack of Bandit, a neighbor's dog named Bear, and a few others named after country stars like Dolly and Jerry Jeff, sent you scrambling back inside like a hunted goat.

That was until one of the dogs, Dr. Michaels' Great Pyrenees, a massive, thickly coated, immensely powerful white sheepdog named "Great White" or GW, tracked down my friend Stevie in the front yard during a game of football. GW clamped down on Stevie's right butt cheek so hard that he moved to Michigan a year later. Our friend's mom made him pull his pants down to show her the mark, and GW got put down.

This was lucky for GW since my dad said he was cooking up an "enhanced sedative" for the whole lot of them after they'd torn through our trash one morning. GW's demise brought peace to the neighborhood but broke Dr. Michaels, who disbanded the bologna and ham rituals before moving a year later.

Bandit returned to our yard and became a rotten house dog, something my dad wouldn't allow before. It's how I knew he was scared of thunder when, before the other dogs' howls would drown out through the rain, Bandit would huddle close, scratching his way under a chair or couch and whimper until someone slid a tennis ball for him to munch.

Now my parents have dogs more for the company than anything. Daisy is a golden lab, named after Gatsby's ill-witted love interest, and Bulleit is a springer spaniel named after bourbon, which my dad doesn't drink.

I buried Scout and Paul Revere in the side yard cemetery a few years ago, side by side, their heavy cold bodies rolled into the shallow holes I'd dug in the rain. Both wrapped in black trash bags. I thought to myself, I guess this is as good as you can expect. They were *just* dogs.

When my mom called years before that, right before a final exam wrapping up my first year of law school, her voice was a sustained, somber whisper. She had something to tell me. She'd call a few years later to tell me my friend Clay had passed away, but this was the first time I'd heard such a severe, quiet tone.

"Casey," she said. "I don't know how to tell you this, but we've had a horrible storm the last three days. Hasn't stopped raining, almost blew the willow over, right out of the roots."

"Okay…" I said, lingering on the willow I'd planted and would often grab thin branches from so my dad could pop me for mouthing off or selling Accelerated Reader quiz points in middle school.

"Well, you know, Bandit is blind and can't really hear either. Well, we can't find him. We think he just went into the woods or something… to die. Dogs do that."

I didn't feel a lump in my throat so much as in my back. It crawled through my lungs, and I felt like I might not come up for air. So much of my life's philosophy wrapped in one little dog that didn't even get a black trash bag and a place in the side yard cemetery.

"Well, can you look for him?"

"It's still raining, Casey. It's so cold. It's been three days. I'm sorry. I haven't even told Leigh. I thought you'd care more."

Cold in east Texas isn't like Louisiana's, where I live now. Texas is sharp and dry. Pine needles turn into darts when it sleets or snows, the pinecones prickly IUDs for an unaware sledder. They call any chill weather movement a "wintery mix" in south Louisiana, and we got a few days off school that week for just such an occurrence. We hosted a "Winter Mix-er" during the worst night, a balmy 54-degree sludge of heavy rain and mud mixed with a 32-degree forecast that never showed.

ꝏ

I wrote a short story about Bandit's death that I turned into a former professor at LSU the following week. After I didn't hear back for a few days, I called to see how she was doing and how she liked the story. Her secretary answered and told me, through that same sustained, somber whisper, that Professor Leiby's car slid across the wintery mix the week before, and she hit a tree. She was dead.

This professor was the editor of a prestigious literary journal on campus, one of the only non-sports related prestigious things about the university, really. She gave me my first publishing credit and even wrote me a letter of recommendation I still use today. She made us read *The Great Gatsby* three times in one semester just because it was the only story she saw worth learning from, and she bought a gun for hurricane season then told us about burying it in her backyard once her power went out because she'd rather an intruder kill her than have to kill somebody. She was funny like that; a sort of neurotic honesty and I stole some of her teaching persona when I started a few years later. She made us write about what we knew and loved in her class, and it was there I realized I couldn't stop writing about this girl I knew and loved but wasn't dating—in fact, she'd left me at our only date, a football game in the driving rain—but would end up being my wife. Things usually improve for me if I'm not wearing a rain poncho.

I had to ask the secretary, "Was she alone?"

"Yes," she said back, breathing hard into the phone's mouthpiece. "Thank. God. I'm sorry you heard it like *this,* but I've been telling everyone that calls. Do you want me to pass the story along to another professor?"

"Well, actually, it's about a quasi-teacher I had, that also died, in the rain, alone. Like a week ago, now that I'm saying it out loud. So—"

The phone clicked off. I don't know where Professor Jeanne Leiby is buried, but here's to hoping she got at least a garbage bag.

Beauty Queen Fight Night

We always met at the park to play basketball, or drink, during breaks in college. The hoops' rims were the thick, unforgiving orange loops that would've made Kobe Bryant give up shooting. My friend Edward was the tallest, maybe 6'3, and the only one with any God-given ability. He'd glide around our chubby frames, the ball skipping effortlessly on the concrete court, and lay it just over the rim. The rest of us were resigned to loud head fakes and chunking jumpers that either ricocheted off the rim or hit off the steel backboard—causing a vibration that the community college's seismograph might pick up. I specifically remember Brian, who was built like our school's lunch lady, slipped on a patch of pine needles mid-shot, the ball hung in the air like a deflated balloon until dropping straight into the net—our only pure swish of the day.

Bringle Lake Park was an almost entirely concrete slab of parking lots, basketball courts, playgrounds, and walking paths on the south end of a small lake with an even smaller green space of browning grass near a sand volleyball court. A small dock stretched over the water, always surrounded with just enough moss to make fishing a chore. It was popular destination for family walks, group birthday parties, and high school dispute resolutions. You might hear about an argument in first period, then before the bell rang for seventh, it was confirmed: "They're going to Bringle."

You'd have to pull off next to an E-Z Mart gas station and follow a winding road until the pavement gave out to rocks, then dirt, then pavement again when you hit the pine-shaded parking lot. This was all in the early 2000s—I hear the new four-year college has a dormitory setup on the park now.

That day was calm. Summer break was coming to an end, and I was growing impatient to get back to college. Geese were playing on the lake, a newly constructed retainer wall had some rather artful graffiti, and Edward was adding to his already lofty pick-up game legacy when the growl of glasspacks and ripped mufflers roared over the treetops.

We let the ball bounce away into the sand of the volleyball court and walked to the edge of the parking lot when a small blue coupe sprung from the tree line, churning up a cloud of dust, its spoiler shining in the sun, its frame bouncing with the bass of its speakers. A glasspack is a cheap muffler that is illegal in the U.K. and generally frowned upon in polite society. You can hear it before you see it. Usually a little red tube, I presume glass, that looks more like a dog's penis than an intimidating car accessory, but that didn't stop a ton of kids in my hometown from sticking it on their sedans, trucks, and SUVs. I thought I'd graduated from the sound a when I moved to Baton Rouge for college, but a guy in my fraternity had a glasspack on his 2002 Mitsubishi Montero Sport. He was from Shreveport, so that checked out.

The blue car ran up onto the asphalt parking lot, the engine eating into the serenity of the nearby geese playdate, and a gaggle of other cars followed out of the woods.

A black Honda Civic, a couple of Camrys, a few trucks of different make a model but mostly Ford Rangers, and one red sedan. The blue coupe found a parking spot across the lot from us and sat rumbling under the threaded shade of a small willow tree. As the other cars filed in, they all made sure to give the blue car a parking spot or two of distance. Doors opened and slammed, and the crowd made their way to the pavilion by the greenspace.

"Well, damn," Brian said, breaking any concentration we had on the scene. "I thought we were about to get to see something."

"Yeah," I said, "Who are these kids?"

"I don't know," someone said, "Look like they might be juniors? Maybe sophomores?" The soft bounce of the ball returned as Edward retrieved it and started shooting. The kids were all under the darkened pavilion, probably for a birthday party or just a meet up. If they were sophomores then they'd just gotten their licenses, and when you just get your license in Texarkana, you feel like you can do just about anything.

I turned to get back to our game when I heard a familiar voice, raspy and wet, yell out, "Casey—hey!"

I turned to find Neil Riley, the younger brother of a friend. He and his brother both had shaved heads since they were young for their swim team. Neil was jogging over in shorts and a long white t-shirt. We exchanged some form of a handshake that came more naturally to me back then, and I asked what they were up to.

"Oh, man, dude, there's gonna be a fight," he said. His voice was always coarse, like he'd been screaming over a dirt bike race the hour before he met you. "Big fight. Gonna be a good one."

I asked who they were—Neil went to Texas High, a 5A school on the other side of town. They had a few D1 scholarship football players that I'm sure knew their way around a punch—but before he could answer, the familiar crunch of gravel turned our attention to the entrance.

A black car, going closer to Mach-5 than whatever the parking lot speed limit might've been, zoomed past us to the end of the asphalt, near the water's edge. The crowd under the pavilion screamed when the car drove by and they started coming out into the sun, huddling around the vibrating blue one.

The black car then reversed back up the hill, its engine whirring like a baseball card stuck in a bike tire. Neil leaned over to me and yelled, "It's Mandy McCoy. She goes to Arkansas High. Just won Miss Teen Texarkana on the Arkansas side!"

"Oh," I said, "That's exciting stuff." I shrugged a little. Another fight over a guy, probably a welder's apprentice or aspiring roughneck. His name was likely Cole, Rhett, or Travis. Or Trent. It was one of those. And these two girls were probably the type that at least pretended they liked to hunt and could drive a stick shift or something.

"And what's going on here?" I said, pointing to the blue car. "Is that the other one? I mean, you know, like the other woman, the mistress or something?"

"Ah, nah, man," Neil said, the black car getting closer and closer, backing into a spot, trunk facing the pavilion. The crowd encircled the two cars, the blue one's stereo still blaring, subwoofers threatening to tip it over. "Mandy was talking shit about *her* dad," Neil said while he pointed from the black to the blue. And before I could run through all the scenarios of what someone would have to say about my dad to get in a fist fight at Bringle Lake, he answered it for me: "Who just died… from cancer!"

The shock of this moment hit me harder back then. Now I'm almost 33 and my glutes feel like death might come tomorrow—just have to hope it's in a more dignified manner than an incurable debilitating illness. Something like a heart attack at the mall. Something my kids won't have to defend in combat, apparently.

He shouted this last part as a door of the blue car flew open, and out came Callie Clausen scratching and screaming like a cat out of water. Her tiny, tan legs propelled her across the parking lot as her short brown ponytail popped back and forth like a towel in gym class. She went to Pleasant Grove, my alma mater. A smaller, white flight 3A school at the time with nothing to its name but a solid volleyball reputation and decent enough ACT averages. Her older sister was my sister's age and on the drill team—another feather in the cap at the school.

Somewhere in her car, I knew she had her Miss Teen Texarkana-Texas sash she'd won a few days earlier. And, yes, her dad had recently passed away. I think from cancer.

Callie started beating on the black car's hood, standing in the way in case it wanted to take off. I couldn't see through the tinted windows, but I imagined this pint-sized pageant queen was putting on a good enough show to scare almost anyone. Then Callie kicked the front headlight. The car turned off, doors opened, and out came four girls. They were thrashing, pulling, and gnawing on Callie in the blink of an eye.

There were a few well-timed accusations like, "Nobody kicks my fuckin' car," while the one I assumed to be Mandy was kicking Callie on the ground, and "I'm gonna fuck up your fuckin' face," while Callie was scratching Mandy's face.

The three other girls from Mandy's car got pulled off by a group of guys at the beginning but would sneak their way back in for a kick or punch. The guys chaperoning would grab them from the waist and sling them out of the way, telling them *we'd* keep this fair. It always went like this. These guys would police the events and decide the winner. They'd pick the villain, ironically missing their part in the affair.

I couldn't breathe the entire scene. Each smear of blood, ripped tank top, or pulled strand of hair widened my eyes a bit more. Mandy's blond hair was pulled out by its black roots.

The summer sun was beating down, and I knew from twisting my ankle and sitting in the grass earlier that it was sharp and hot. They were rolling in it. Neil was standing on a picnic table now, screaming "Get her!" His arms pointing to the sky like Rocky Balboa in the purest, most East Texas form of ecstasy I can imagine.

At one point, Callie got Mandy onto her back and landed a few open palmed tiger paws across her blushed face, dirty from makeup, blood, and grass. One of Mandy's gang, who I was instinctively—if not from school pride then from my love of the underdog—growing to hate, tackled Callie to the ground. The girl was dragged out of the fray by her shorts by Neil and another guy, but it gave Mandy enough time to roll over and secure a solid grip on Callie's ponytail. Then the real yanking started.

She about broke Callie's neck as she paraded her around the pavement, Callie swiping from her back, Mandy tugging on the ponytail with her right hand, running in a haphazard circle, punching wildly with the left. Callie tried to roll over but, from the looks of things, Mandy had been in a scrap or two—I think Scrapping was a credited elective course at Arkansas High—and she dropped a knee into Callie's back. She pinned her on the ground and gave a few pops to the ear before the sound of sobs outdid the crowd, the cussing, and the still vibrating car.

When Mandy got up and stepped back, we could see Callie lying in a fetal lump. Her volleyball shorts were torn or scuffed beyond recognition, and her hair went every which way like she'd just been electrocuted by the sophistication of the moment. If this were a hidden camera moment on ABC's show *What Would You Do?* which I've now spent hours dissecting the actions of others in the face of controversy or shame, I failed the test.

She sat up on her side like a mermaid, yelled that Mandy was a b-word, which Mandy trumped with a c-word, before the less than empathetic crowd climbed in their cars, leaving her in the dirt and the grass and the concrete and blood. She was stoic for a moment, like a waylaid, duty-bound foot soldier. She had to fight, had to, despite the overbearing sense of loss and fruitless outcomes—like a service academy football player going into face Alabama.

Neil ran over and gave me a fist-pound before leaving. "Man, that was incredible. Glad you got to see that, huh?" He was jumping back and forth like he'd just had too much Mountain Dew.

"I guess so. Holy shit," is all I could muster.

"See ya, man," he said over his shoulder, a group motioning him to a large truck. "I'll tell Mikey you said Hey!"

"No," I said, "Don't tell anyone I was here."

The cars took off, and the sounds of their engines, the gravel, and the stereos were replaced again by the dribbling basketball, clanging backboard, and vibrating windows of the blue coupe. Callie was now sitting with her legs crossed well enough that I remembered she was a gymnast. Her elbows sat on her knees, hands holding her head up a little as she looked at the ground, moaning on and off. She had a helpless confidence about her as if she might cry or punch the ground.

I turned to find Edward still dribbling, absent from the theater of cruelty. Brian and Adam stood in shocked silence. I doubt even this stopped Edward from playing basketball. Brian and I walked, our hands in gym shorts, over to the blue car. Brian reached in and turned the music off, which drew her attention to us. Her glare was lessened by the fact her left eyebrow, which must've been draw on pre-brawl, was gone, and her face and left ear were reddish but not mangled. She had a busted bottom lip, and her shoulder, bare from the ripped tank top, was slowly dripping like through a cheese cloth.

"You okay?" I asked. I winced when she looked at me, her hair was matted down with some cocktail of sweat, grass, and blood, and the right side of her neck that I couldn't see before had a bad gash, the hint of highlighter-green nail polish around the mark. It's the image that flashes in my mind every time the all-girls Catholic school in town sends us a letter. *Academic Excellence! Blue Ribbon Award Winning!* But dammit if girls can't be brutal. Today I hold my daughter close—knowing that soon someone will be equally as cruel, but hopefully just with fists and not words. Bruises wear off, and makeup can cover a scratch, but little girls are starting to scare the shit out of me. I can still smell the blood from Callie's knees, an odor like copper—like a bowl of pennies.

It's not lost on me that Callie went to my high school which was split down the middle with boys and girls, and there I'd been, letting it happen.

"Do I look okay?" she said.

I felt bad. We knew the Clausens, and I knew my dad had done something at the hospital during the treatments—something positive, I'm assuming—but I wished I could be a similar help now. What should I say to a beauty pageant queen that just got drug around a parking lot by another beauty queen because she showed up to fight in the name of cancer-shaming?

"You look like you just got pulled around a parking lot by your hair," Brian said, covering the general gist of what I was thinking.

"Well fuck you," she said and got up, pebbles and dirt falling to the ground as she wiped her shorts and legs. She climbed into her car, slammed the door shut, and the doors and windows went back to vibrating. She backed up quickly, nearly missing Brian's foot, and screeched out of Bringle Lake Park.

"Can you believe that, man?" I said, my hands held out in front of me like I was trying to catch some rain. "What the hell was that?" Brian shook his head as we walked back to the court. "And what's she getting mad at us for?" I grappled with the idea that maybe we should've intervened. What would that dude from *Apocalypto*—a movie I'd recently seen and decided was worth structuring my idea of chivalry and honor around—have done? He'd of grabbed a poisonous frog, rigged a dart gun out of one of these cat tail reeds, and shot Mandy. So, that was out. "Aren't you mad she told us to fuck off?"

Brian laughed. "Nope." He called for the ball. "She's embarrassed. And I'd bet fighting wasn't her talent at the pageant."

We all laughed. Looking at my daughter now who, at three and a half, didn't put up much a fight during the local Methodist Church's Easter Eucharist and Egg hunt last week, I feel it's safe to surmise she probably wouldn't stand a chance at Bringle Lake. My wife keeps showing me fliers of different after school activities, and try as I might, I can't help but lean towards the gender normative activities for a little girl—something Texarkana people might call "girl sports" like ballet, tennis, or soccer—something European. If she tries softball, will that lead to a scrap? Despite my best efforts, she'll probably be what she wants. My wife will say it's meant to be.

"Besides," Brian said, dribbling the ball quickly from outside the 3-point line "All I can think about right now is draining this shot in your face." In one motion he stepped back and heaved the ball towards the goal—as graceful and smooth as a sneeze. Brian had been a left tackle on the football team in high school and approached every athletic endeavor as such. The ball lined to the square on the backboard, smacked the center and missed the rim. The metal pole attached to the backboard rocked back and forth, the backboard itself rattling like a tin roof in a hurricane. "Shit!" he yelled. "How does Edward keeping making these?"

The Helluv' It

There's a sign outside town, somewhere when the rubber finally meets paved road winding through cleared interstate and a piney curtain of trees and sky, and because it's in Texas and not Arkansas or Louisiana, the road looks relatively new. A blue metallic shimmering sign that probably cost the same amount as the GDP of the town. It's big, so if you're driving fast and blink, you won't miss it. The colors stick out on the blue backdrop—maroon, gold, and a bright, ostentatious orange.

The sign is properly announcing all of the area schools' state championships. Not chess or mathletes or speech and debate, but real sports like football, baseball, basketball, women's volleyball, softball and track and field, in that order. No soccer or swimming, and not because they haven't been won.

Sports rule the area roost. Old men golf, kids join youth leagues of all sorts, one of my mom's friends broke her ankle a while back, from what my mom said, "I think she was just drunk out there playing tennis or something," so it even gets in the mix during a good binge. There's a stark divide between the country club games, the country club kids and the furious, draconian attitude surrounding Texas football.

The coaches range from the Disney movie father figures you might hope to find hosting your son's hot afternoon, to the tobacco spitting, overlapped brow, hiked-up shorts look that somehow always comes with well-developed trap muscles. Coaches would usually go on to become administrators at the schools, sometimes even the community college. I found this generally odd until I myself taught at an all-boys Catholic school in Louisiana, what you might think would be a higher brand of academics but would also substitute former wrestling and golf coaches in for the chaplain or Dean of Discipline—at least it was golf and wrestling, I told myself. Ancient games.

At our Texas schools the practice facilities, the equipment, the uniforms, the production of it all, was tenfold the education department's budget which could be seen by the number of times we read *Lord of the Flies* – three times from sixth grade to senior year. I figured it was just a damn good book – descriptions of friendship, hardship, family, and survival in a wilderness of adolescence hit home with me at eleven and eighteen, but in reality, that's just all we had. Thems the brakes. *Sucks to your Asmar.*

Lo and behold, when I grasped the minds to mold years later at the all-boys Catholic school with the yearly tuition higher than my college payments, I reached for the comfort of the familiar green cover—the blonde boy, twigs and sticks and leaves sticking out of his hair. I actually separated the class into Hunters and Builders, like in the book, and, to my surprise – they tried to kill each other. "I'm not sure what you were expecting," the former football coach turned Dean of Instruction told me after a class melee. He had a point.

Back to the sign, Texas High was the large five-A high school in town (Texas ranks their public schools by the number of asses in seats, one through five), aptly named because it was on the Texas side of town. It'd won a few football state championships over the years and a couple in track and field. It had some impressive alumni that went on the play in the NFL and elsewhere. Wikipedia also credits it with two pornstars. Some of the less-impressive alumni went on to study at places like Notre Dame, Harvard, Stanford, SMU, or cheer in the original iteration of the XFL.

Liberty Eylau is the 3-A, mostly black school on the south side of town and had a few football and baseball championships of its own. Its maroon leopard growled on the blue sign. They had a few Major League Baseball players that I knew personally and one Heisman Trophy candidate that I watched my college team harass and possibly injure in Dallas one year—so who really came out on top there? Once, when we were in the seventh grade, our first sanctioned year of school football, this same kid met us at the 50-yard-line for the coin toss and told a kid named Bo, and I quote, "I'm comin' straight for you – I'm giving you a bo-bo."

"What the hell was he talking about?" Bo asked on our way back from the coin toss – which we'd won. I just shook my oversized helmet back and forth. I was thirteen and besides having to brave *Nightmare on Elm Street* at a Homecoming dance afterparty at my date's house, that coin toss was the scariest thing I'd ever seen. And, to LaMichael's credit, he did come for Bo. Multiple times. Over and over—just kept running him over. To have that physical awareness in seventh grade when half of us were still trying to figure out our cleat size, should've been the first hint I wasn't destined for Cooperstown.

Two of the fastest human beings I'd ever seen went to Liberty Eylau, and most of the white guys were named Ricky.

My high school, the white flight 3-A school to the north, had a ray of success in baseball and football after I graduated. Two state titles in each—both football championships I watched with pride and had my mom order me a commemorative XL championship shirt that I finally accepted wouldn't fit and gave to Goodwill a couple of months ago. There were multiple state championships in baseball and an MLB National League Championship Series MVP whom my coach at the time thought wise to start over me at third base for one game my senior year. "OK, this kid can't possibly be better than me," I'd said, almost laughing at the very idea. Again, I ask who came out on top here.

The same baseball coach would strut around the weight room every morning at our 6:30 workouts counting our reps. He was a fanatic for what he called "aerobic arcane exercises" like jumping jacks. Jumping jacks, if you've never tried, are hell. A silly seizure like rhythm that, on the surface, looks like fun, but after one hundred in a row, test the inside of your thighs more than any motorcycle or rope swing ever good. Coach Ford walked around with a paddle he'd commissioned sculpted out of whatever pine or sycamore made Major League Baseball bats. Birchwood? Ironically, while working for the Chamber of Commerce in Baton Rouge in my thirties, I set up a few deals with the Marucci company that now supplies the MLB's bats and sadistic coaches everywhere with firm, failsafe paddles.

Coach Ford gave us a speech before each season ramped up about a ticket. It was a golden ticket, and only he had it. It was in the back pocket of a pair of coach's shorts, a kind of navy nylon with a waste-band that naturally gravitates above the navel. If you followed his directions, if you listened to him, if you trusted him, and if you worked for him, you'd get the ticket. We would all sit with our legs crossed on the sweaty, slick weight room mat in a crescent moon as he marched back-and-forth in front. He'd again explain the concept of the golden ticket for anyone that hadn't seen or read the Roald Dahl story, periodically asking if we really wanted it. "Yes, coach!" We'd call back, and he'd smirk. Us in our stale athletics shirts with Pleasant Grove Athletics printed on the front and sweat stains crusting into the fabric which smelled, best to my recollection, like sweltering garbage and piss rags, watched open-mouthed as he triumphantly called us in to follow him to the championship. He faked like he might pull it out every now and then, like he might reveal its authenticity, reaching behind and rummaging around in his pocket with a wry, dip-stained grin.

"You want the ticket, don't you O'Banion?" He asked one evening after practice, the mosquitos and gnats gathering around the flood lights shining over the diamond.

"I could go either way," I said.

"Bullshit," he said, laughing and grabbing at his pocket before stopping. "I know y'all want to see it, but I won't show it to you until O'Banion says he wants to see it."

He'd never show you the ticket, but you'd know when you got it, he said.

It was a ticket to the state championship tournament down in Austin. The speech always started off the same with a warning if you don't listen, not only will you not make the state championship, not only will you not win the district, not only will you not live up to your potential on the field and in life, but in a year or two, if you're lucky enough to graduate, you'll be faced with a desperate possibility of intermural fraternity softball. I went home one day after the golden ticket speech and told my mom that damn, I couldn't wait to play intermural softball (I lasted two games on our fraternity team before the LSU Student Recreational officers told me there was no cigarette smoking in the outfield, and our law school team, the Hawaiian shirt clad *Subpoena Coludas*, were a hefty 2-8 in our three years—and I wish you could see how long it just took spell check to figure out I was trying to spell subpoena and not supernatural). Others were a little more ambitious and played community college baseball somewhere for a year or two before transferring to a major college just for, as Coach Ford called it, "the helluvit," which meant to study. Others, like I've mentioned, went on to become professional athletes, playing a game for a living, hanging out with a group of guys for a living, traveling to interesting places for a living—reaching out and grabbing that ticket. The closest I'd get to professional athletics came once year around Christmas, when the Texas Rangers would send some bench players to the Texarkana Central Mall to sign autographs. We'd show up late, bear witness to the line curling around the Limited Too and beyond the Auntie Anne's and turn to go home.

One time at a party out in a field, where parties were usually held, I sat near a large bonfire, its flames stretching into the sky and bursting momentarily each time a bottle of alcohol got thrown into the mix. A friend of mine wanted to introduce me to somebody.

"Casey," he said, "This is *Blaze*."

I balked initially, smiling aimlessly at the name, the spiky gelled hair, and the forearms of what you might assume belonged to a forty-year-old manual laborer, not a little boy named *Blaze*. I would balk again twelve years later when one of my sisters told me she was thinking of naming her son *Blaise* after one of the Saints (from the Bible not New Orleans). "You can't," I said. "It's a dumb name."

With this Blaze though, I shook hands and felt the power of his forearms before looking back into the fire. "Blaze plays baseball at Texas High," my buddy said.

"Oh, nice." I said. "What position?"

"Well," he said with a slight drawl, "Pitch a lil', hit a lil', field a lil'. I do it all. I'm fast as shit, too. Especially for a white boy."

"Let's hope so," I said, shaking my head slightly in the direction of my friend Andrew, whose ears cast shadows from the fire onto the wall of pine trees and raised pickups behind us, his baseball hat pulled down hard so you couldn't see his eyebrows. Our mascot had always been a hawk, and for over twenty years we stole the University of Iowa's Hawkeye logo sitting on Andrew's black hat that night. This was until Iowa's top brass noticed an inundation of merchandise orders from a small town in East Texas, a cease-and-desist letter following. Pleasant Grove caved—unlike the school across the state line. The Arkansas High Razorbacks received a full-blown lawsuit from the University of Arkansas for using the Razorback mascot, but, after a little digging and countersuit, Arkansas High discovered they were using the mascot before the university, so in a fitting restitution, the university has to give the high school all of their athletic equipment when they're finished each season (this was truly a substantial point against the university's law school when I toured it years later).

"Blaze just got drafted," Andrew said.

I have a bad habit of showing people when I'm confused or when I think something merits a facial expression. I scrunch my face, open my mouth, and usually do a short laugh. After gaining a little weight, it's been described as a belly laugh. Really, it's more of like a torso jolt, but it's quick. They'd call me surprisingly athletic if I were at the NFL draft combine and could see my twitching stomach. I made this face when I heard about this *Blaze* being drafted.

Maybe it was the Smirnoff Ice we'd stolen from a friend's mom's cabinet, but I said, "Thanks for your service, I guess?"

"This guy is a fuckin' idiot," Blaze said and walked off.

"No, dip shit," Andrew said, shoving me towards the fire, "Got drafted by the Yankees. In the third round right out of high school. He's a millionaire."

He suddenly appeared again. "Yeah, I recently came into some money, so I decided to buy a new bass boat." This is about when cell phones were able to show only a few pixelated images, and he showed me a fuzzy gray stern that looked like it was the size of an upturned Airstream trailer.

"Is that a nice one?" I asked. My dad would undoubtedly be annoyed with the question but also proud that I didn't know what a *nice* bass boat was compared to a *not nice* bass boat. Would be like knowing the difference between tap water and fridge water – who cares, my dad would say.

"Hell yeah it's a nice bass boat," he said, pointing to a fuzzy picture of the back. "It's got twin engines, twin motors. Two three-fifties. You can take it out in the Gulf, or you can take it out on the lake. And I bought a new truck to haul it. All cash."

"Oh, wow," I said. "I didn't know they were a lot of lakes in New York." Again, the Smirnoff getting the best of my stomach and my face. I still couldn't get over the name Blaze.

"You're funny," he said, "But that shits gonna get you in trouble one day."

ൕ

It did end up getting me in trouble. The next year, my senior year, our saint of an English teacher, Mrs. Campbell, gave us an assignment: write a letter to one person in the school that had made a big difference in our lives (this was the non-advanced English class. I dropped the advanced class after the first day when a friend was drug into the hall by his ear for laying his head down and telling the teacher he was an auditory learner). Me and my friend Sandy decided in and ill-timed first attempt at satire, to write to Coach Ford to explain he'd been like a father to us. As a result, we were forced to run two miles every day after practice until we "got faster." And we were forced to sit out, or is he put it, "pop a quarter in the pine pony," during a weekend tournament in Shreveport.

We played three teams that were vying for the Louisiana state championship that year, one of which came from all the way from Baton Rouge in two coach buses—one for their luggage. It was an all-boys Catholic school, the same I'd teach at nine years later. We were told not to speak the entire trip, so even when the P.A. announcer came down to the dugout to ask the coach how to pronounce a few different names, I wasn't allowed to correct him when he got to O'Banion. "That one right there wont be an issue. Trust me," Coach Ford said. And even when that P.A. announcer asked if I was Dennis O'Banion's son, explaining he'd known my dad from college and med school, and had a son and daughter my age (that I would later get to know and the daughter would be my wife's maid of honor), I was given a universal sign to zip my lips via Coach Ford yelling, "Shut the fucking hell up," before my mouth opened. I see the P.A. announcer every now and then and I don't think he remembers it. Just one of those funny little moments where your mouth writes a check your ass can't cash, Coach Ford told me.

We had soccer players in town, we had boxers, and some great cross-country runners. Hell, my sister dated a guy for a while that also got drafted in the third round of Major League Baseball draft and went on to play for over ten years. Tiger Woods came through town and won a tournament at the Texarkana Country Club. There were semi-professional golfers and tennis stars—who knew there was so much money in golf and tennis coaching? Not me until I saw all the white kids playing it.

For every athlete there was a parent. Some parents that were going to watch practice. And the parents that were going to bring Sonic milkshakes to the coaches every day during practice to make sure the coaches knew their sons had been hitting extra balls in the batting cage. I always wondered if their kids liked their parents around so much, but now I wonder what those men did for a living to accomplish such an enviable work-life balance and pay the air conditioning bill at the same time.

Then there were the parents that were going to print out a 100-page binder, laminated, with graphs and charts and photo evidence showing their son's swing is without a doubt a one in a million match to 2005's Albert Pujols—his MVP year. That happened once when we were somewhere, a hot and dry baseball tournament. The school got us motel rooms to cool down in between games, one of those with the vending machines that only have cans and you can press them against your forehead until your brain cools down.

Laying on a bed with at least three other guys, a dad charged in, roused the couch, and flipped through a binder in the midday heat, the whirring of the window unit in the motel sputtering and spitting over their data driven discourse. Sandy and our friend John David looked at me as the dad, Mr. Black, showed an overlay of his sixteen-year-old, 145-pound son and a 220-pound adult man, pre-whatever arthritis comes with your first divorce, Albert Pujols swinging.

"See, see, see, his swing is just like it. It's just like Carsyn's. So, he needs to be batting third just like Albert."

"Did you say Albert Pujols?" I asked, leaning over the nightstand. Coach Ford glanced up from the shimmering pages, glossy in his hands, and had a sort of smile that I got periodically when he knew where I was going. He probably would've put up with it, too, but he liked being doted on more than he liked me.

"Yeah, that's what I said," Mr. Black said. He was a young dad for having a kid my age, but I thought all parents were young compared to my own. His hair was always wet and slicked back, and he was the first person, I recall seeing at least, that wore tennis shoes with a suit – I'm thinking he must've been a drug rep or something. The binders make more sense with an erectile disfunction pill or a big translucent penis overlaying a soft, sagging one.

"Come on – I thought you said Albert Pujols, and you're completely right! We've been saying that for years, me and the guys. Carsyn is a budding Albert Pujols.

"Get the hell out of here, O'Banion," Coach Ford said with a straight face, spitting a dribble of chew into a Coke can and placing it back on the wonky linoleum nightstand next to my elbow, its content's scent floating up to my nose just long enough to whiff the thick peppermint.

I rolled off the bed and headed towards the door.

"Why don't you take your friends with you?" Mr. Black said. John David and Sandy threw their arms up in protest.

"What'd we do?" they asked.

"You don't need to be listening in on this conversation," Mr. Black said. It's always been one of those conversations, one of those situations in time that you think about what you could've said, what you should've said. What would land the biggest impact? In every hypothetical dreamed up scenario, your response is better than it was in real life.

"All right, Mr. Black," I said. "We're leaving." I should've made mention that he wasn't actually on the high school baseball team—which the room, according to the duct taped paper sign on the door and allocated reimbursement in the school board's budget, was reserved for.

"You know," Mr. Black said, his back turned to the door, "You guys have a lotta promise, lotta talent. You're from good stock—you should just shut your mouth every now and then and you might play a little more… learn something, even from the younger guys like Carsyn."

"I'm not playing a lot because of what's going into my mouth, not what's coming out." Coach and Mr. Black glanced at each other, I could see in the soft glow of the yellow lamp they didn't get it. "Too slow, I said laughing, "I'm eating too much. Your son's playing 'cause what's going into yours." I wish I'd thought of that last part.

That same dad would confront me and John David in the bathroom mid-urinal stream a couple of weeks later to tell us to leave his son alone and to stop joking with him or it was going be the end of our baseball playing days, he'd to make sure of it. Little did he know, our baseball days would end a couple weeks later in the playoffs after I made two errors. I find hindsight is always 20/20 when you're threatening children.

ꝏ

A minor-league hockey team started in Texarkana around 2004. There was a big vote in the paper to decide the name of the team: it came down to the Fire Ants versus The Border City Bandits, a raccoon with a hockey jersey on, biting into a stick. They played at the Four States Fairground Arena, the same place we had the annual Toughman Tri-state Tournament, and the same place I once threw up on the UFO gravity ride at the fair, and their players, mercenary high schoolers from Minnesota, Wisconsin, and something called "the DAHkoTAS" went to our white flight school. In that sense, when you count the socio-economic status from free lunches to free range chicken lunches brought by moms in the newly minted limited Toyotas and Mercedes, and mix in the soccer playing foreign exchange contingent, and the hockey kids, Pleasant Grove High School was quite possibly the most diverse predominately white school in the country. There were even a few Jewish and Catholic kids.

Earlier I mentioned it didn't seem like high school athletics changed much. I recall teaching at the all-boys Catholic school in Baton Rouge and how the large donations went to new athletic facilities—a new wrestling mat, new baseball bats, or a new shower, which I found particularly troubling. Sure, some went to a recording studio for the budding artists that lined the halls, and some went to a new student center with sponsors like fast food restaurants and car dealers. But as for the humanities budget, we were back to the tattered, broken back copies of William Golding's 1954 masterpiece about kids surviving and passing time between exercises of futility in adolescence, adulthood, and death.

Paris, Texas

My mom attempted to replace me with a foreign exchange student from Switzerland my junior year of high school. A good time to want me out of the house, to her credit. For the first couple of months, Nias (pronounced Knee-Us) spoke broken English and carried a Toblerone bar to hand to people as a chocolate peace offering.

A 6'2 blonde kid with a gelled mo-hawk and capri pants—always capri pants and white Puma shoes—Nias grew in popularity in our house, the school, and the soccer team. Blue-eyed, his face was pock-marked from pimples that seemed more like scars from a Swiss banking inside job than pre-teen mutation.

He got his driver's license after applying for a permit his second week in the states, passing the test before I could, and he was best remembered behind the wheel of my family's 1998 cherry red suburban, which had a mouse running around in it for the better part of the six months that Nias and I drove it, screaming down the dusty side roads, blasting whatever hip hop or outlandish country music CD he could get his hands on. He loved pulling in a driveway or school parking lot with dip spit flying out the window he'd smile, a kind of crooked European grin, and yell "How-dee!"

I was forced to drive him and the other foreign exchange students—a girl from Germany and a guy from Columbia—to school and the mall for the first semester. Once Nias procured the license and got the keys to the Suburban, they were released on the town, especially the Texarkana Central Mall. Nias took me and the German girl, Manja, multiple times. She would go on to date my friend Clint our senior year, before they broke up the next summer on a street corner in Munich. Manja was a leather model in Germany. I didn't find out until we watched her try on prom dresses at the Dillard's in the mall, what a leather model in Germany really looks like. Me, a 5'10 pushing 5'11 maturing dork eating a handful of Chic-Fil-A fries, and Nias, a gangly Swiss ultra dork who, when he laughed, spit out of his top front teeth, watched her try on between ten to twenty dresses while my buddy Cheeseburger's mom, Mrs. Penny, stood in the corner and burst into a nodding fit each time Manja exited the dressing room. "Oh, no, honey. No, no. No way—you can-not wear that in public. I don't even see why I got it for you. Honey, no!"

Famous for hooking up with Miss Teen Texarkana, my older sister's friend, which people thought impressive for someone speaking something as harsh as German, Nias could also win any boxing match, including once choking me out over the depleting Toblerone stash. My mom also instituted a fun rule where if I was grounded, Nias was also grounded, and vice versa. So, when my grades were bad, we sat at the table, Nias and my dad joking about when I'd pull my proverbial head out of my proverbial ass so they could get some beer for dinner. When Nias struggled in Advanced Calculus—a subject, mind you, that doesn't require much English to master—my mom made him Swiss Bundt Cakes and Swiss rolls and some sort of Swiss pudding. But the greatest gift he gave Texarkana was taking me and two friends, Edward and Cody, to Europe for the first time. We were the first of anyone I knew that had really been to Europe outside of a school sanctioned senior trip that went to Italy every year... until multiple Baptist kids demanded to take communion at the Vatican.

We watched the movie *Hostel* on the way over, and I sat erect in two ways for twelve hours as I imagined the possibility of being kidnapped and the dilemma that I would have of what body part to lose first, or if I would be so overpowered by the joy of having sex that I wouldn't care.

We landed in Saint Gallen, Switzerland just outside of Zürich, a beautiful, rolling green town, small but every inch of it a luscious, expensive, and historic valley. We sat, jetlagged but excited as Nias's mom, Claudia (pronounced like *cloud* not Claude) who had not visited him in the states, took us to what she called the village's "prize for American interests" – a textile factory that sent merchandise over on the Mayflower. Edward fell asleep in the middle of the tour, sitting in an old weaver's chair, leaning against the chiseled stone walls of the thatched hut. It was either the sewing or threading process that did him in. Claudia stopped the entire tour to scold Edward and call us a nasty group of Americans. I've never been so confused or more confident that I wouldn't get kidnapped but more so given away. She was a tightly wound woman that dressed each morning in pant suits or the starched version of Nias's signature capris. She wore her dark blond hair short, like a football helmet, and no jewelry of any kind.

She rarely smiled but often doted on Nias, his younger brother Timo, and any girl that stayed with Nias during the week we spent in St. Gallen.

We finally got to their house that night which looked like something out of a modern Hansel and Gretel. Straight and sterile white walls, but each morning a man with a "big ole horn," as I told my mom, blew a tune from the grass covered cliffs nearby. Timo was named after the island where his parents conceived him, similar to Nias.

Timo reminds me of my two-year-old son if I gave him an enema of Red Bull. Looking back, my diagnosis would be an advanced form of attention deficit dynamite. He was around fifteen or so and screamed whenever he spoke, particularly in English. He called LeBron James a lazy fool. I was not and have never been a big fan of LeBron James, but it's accurate to suggest there was no truer fanatic of LeBron James that week than me in a Swiss basement hearing about how a Swiss athlete could easily handle him one-on-one.

The second day we slept in, which annoyed Claudia and Wolfgang. Nias's dad was a squatty man with a round belly and pleasing smile wrapped by a graying mustache. He'd been on the Swiss downhill ski team before meeting Claudia and was now a speeding ticket attorney. Later that week, they'd take us hiking up the Alps and bring only seltzer water (what we only knew at the time as "water with bubbles") which caused multiple stops along the majestic mountain path (When we reached the top, there was "real milk," which, again, we didn't understand and drank freely until again relieving ourselves on the way down).

Access to the bathroom was denied, or at least the one shower, so we had to take baths to get ready for our trip to Zürich the first day. They were going to show us the Autobahn and what European city life was like. We took two cars—Edward and I climbed in with Nias and Claudia, and Cody got into a cramped two-door wagon with Wolfgang, who seemed a little more accepting of the sleepy Americans, and Timo. Traveling at about 100 miles an hour down the Autobahn, we were regaled with the many benefits of Swiss life: European culture, the value of a Franc, and the illustrious strategy of non-complacent, subtle defiance during World War II and how that, and not any efforts amongst the Allies, resulted in the Nazi collapse.

We finally arrived in Zürich and were scolded about how if we hadn't slept in until 9:30, we would've gotten to see "our Disney castle," that the famous one is based on in Orlando. Instead, we ran around shops and watched the family sort through enormous bags of rice. Which kind of rice did they want? Which bag? Which merchant? "Slap this bag, Ca-sec,"

Wolfgang would suggest, presenting a large bag of basmati. I'd slap the bag and he'd listen intently, his ear on the twined bag like a seashell.

Wolfgang tried pitting two rice merchants against each other but failed. Then it was decided there would be no rice purchasing until we'd seen all the rice the Eastern bloc had to offer. Nias whispered with his mom the whole time until he beckoned to me.

"Follow us—I think you'll like this more," he said.

We went with him, Timo, and Claudia to a lingerie store where they picked out a bra and thong for their mother, making sure to hold them up to her rigid pant-suited frame and announce the ones that would please their father, saying things like, "This will please him!" and imitating Wolfgang growing a boner.

And thus, marked my first and last in-person lingerie shopping experience, as I told my wife the morning of our fifth anniversary when she opened up a laced nightgown from Amazon.

We did this all while hung over with jetlag, bellies empty except various fruit jams—all they provided for breakfasts because, "that's what Americans like." After rice and thong shopping, we went back to St. Gallen. Cody could be seen through their car window performing an exaggerated screaming, scratching distress signal against the back window as they passed. An attempt at a joke in a troubling, fast-paced, scary time, and the hardest I'd laughed in days. They wanted us to take a Gondola to the top of a mountain the next day, but Cody was deathly afraid of heights. When we ran the bleachers in middle school P.E., he had to run up the children's bleachers on the side of the football bleachers—had a note from a doctor and everything, so we all said we'd rather do something else that day. Wolfgang took a long drag of his cigarette before slamming his fist on the outdoor breakfast table amongst a swell of dewy grass and morning fog. "I cannot," he said, "imagine living my life without being to the top of a mountain. It is a cowardly thing you are doing," he said, and as if to drive the point home, he pointed directly at Cody, who was eating a spoonful of grape jelly. "You have not lived until you've seen the world from atop a mountain. You cannot say you've lived."

"I'd rather die on the ground," Cody said.

The next week they shipped us out of the house, off to Paris. There, we would watch the World Cup—the famous French headbutt year—but we saw the game before which France won 1-0. We ran the streets shouting French phrases we'd just learned until people caught on that we were American and threw us out of various cafes and bars. One moment an elderly man was kissing Edward's cheek, spewing tears and what I assumed was praise for the good old boys in blue; the sound of clinking glasses and air horns (this was a few years before the vuvuzelas introduction) rang throughout the bar and something that tasted an awful lot like Coors Lite filled the glasses. The lights flickered with the sheer blur or noise and the white walls of the bar grew wet with the tears and beer and spittle from the riot of happiness. It was a splendid time. This was until the old man paused to hear Edward's take on the game. "I'm American!" he yelled back and met a crash of open palmed slaps that sent us to the door, Nias wailing with laughter—remending us of the French's futile defense of the Nazis once we got out to the baren but static streets.

My mom had gifted me a small camera with one battery. "Take pictures of the Eiffel Tower," she'd said. "Take pictures of the Colosseum. Take pictures of the food you eat!" I'd been taking pictures of what they called a Double Quarter Pounder. The rest of the pictures were from the night France beat Portugal—a blurry kaleidoscope of blue, red, beer, twinkling streetlights, and three Americans and one Swiss running around making a mockery of the sacred game.

I was too hung over to focus at the Louvre, and we had to move—that day the Swiss Family Robinson had set us up with a friend of theirs. A Swiss ex-pat and newly canonized French citizen, Elfie, a tour guide in Paris, was going to show us the town like we'd never dreamed. We met her at her flat, a small but comfortable room just over a white clothed restaurant. My kids love the movie *Ratatouille*, and the restaurant was one I imagine those rats would covet—a café with a trellis of vines growing up to red and white stripped cloth awning hanging over the outdoor tables, the sound of a woman's voice humming melodramatic over an accordion and piano, a baroque but simple scene. Her flat had books and couches crammed into every corner, with plush, round pillows to sit on. Everything was a deep maroon or gold, and the sun coming through the windows emphasized the dust coming off the furniture, floating through the room like the smell of croissants from below.

Elfie told us that we would go see the Eiffel Tower, the Champs-Élysées, and the Arc de Triomphe. She spoke using her body like an Italian's hands, and stood at attention, her arms pointing to the flat's ceiling, touching just above her head as she excitedly yelled, "The Eiffel Tower!" then she marched in place and saluted during "the Champs-Élysées and Arc de Triomphe!" Her nose had a perfect miniscule wart on the front left, which gave her a delightfully eccentric quality. Petite framed, she had to be under five feet, and she seemed not to mind the nickname Elfie. She wore voluminous blue and white striped overalls with small brown canvas shoes which made her glide across the streets.

"Wait out front," she said. "I'll be right around with *our ride*," and she giggled as she reached into her bag and pulled out a blue and white train conductor's cap and fastened it over her plump head. The twigs of brown hair sticking out the side of the cap bent to the sky and she did a little hop, pointing again to the ceiling.

We went outside and she skipped around the corner. Before anyone could ask what was going on, we heard a sharp *ding ding.* From around the side came a full-fledged golf cart train, four cars in length. The front golf cart was shaped like an old coal train engine with golden piping around a white canvas and a small padded stool to sit and look out the window with an open back. The second and third cars had small doors and side windows but looked real enough like you might jump in one at Disney World. Then the caboose, which had a caricature of her face on the side, and two small benches facing one another. She pulled down a small microphone, swinging the train in front of us. Amidst giggles, she announced on crackling speakers running over the cart roofs, "Ok, boys! Do you have your tickets?" She reached into the ceiling and pulled a small cord that rang a bell. *Ding! Ding!*

We were all laughing, apprehensively dumfounded except for Nias who, I assume out of some devotion to former countryman, knew he needed to act like the grownup. He sat in the second car while the rest of us piled into the caboose.

The streets of Paris whizzed by—the shops and bars in the twilight hours of the day. I don't know the exact date, but I know that Elfie on her microphone could yell out sights like the Nike store, Louis Vuitton, and Lacoste—we had Lacoste in our mall! "There's where we ate lunch!" she yelled, where the wine cost less than the water, I remember. We flew under the Eiffel Tower, weaving around the sidewalks and lawns right up to the iron concourse. Cody, again, was not up for taking the elevator to the top.

We wheeled around a corner, and Elfie's voice whistled a tune through the train's P.A. system. Slowly we emerged from the greenery around the tower and entered a large shadow sprawling across the pavement of what seemed to be an enormous roundabout.

"And here is the magnifique Arc de Triomphe!" Elfie cried over the squeal of thirty-two golf cart tires and a chorus of honks. The ancient concrete structure blushed in the waning sun, and I was taken with the stillness. It was quite possibly the largest physical structure I'd seen at that point in my life—sure the Texas Giant rollercoaster at the Dallas Six Flags Amusement Park was taller, but the girth of the Arc stilled me. It was here I thought of the tallest building in Texarkana might be the state prison or maybe a bank. Both lacked the ornate industrialism of this piece of rock in front of me now. The thought would linger for approximately fifteen more seconds before my attention was diverted.

We continued around the circle until a long traffic lined street opened up, cut straight into the city sprawl as if by a bottle rocket. The caboose whipped into line behind the rest of the train and we were now stretched across the entire road as Elfie deftly maneuvered the twenty-four-foot snake into traffic. We came to an abrupt stop.

There's nothing in the world that brings you back to reality quicker than traffic. I realized we were blocking all western bound traffic on the Champs-Élysées. Cars lined up behind us on the roundabout, and cross traffic halted, their bumpers so close we could feel the wind beneath each honk. We only knew a few French soccer phrases, but I understood the universal language of pure, unadulterated hatred for the tourists in the tiny golf cart train blocking what might be the busiest street in the world.

"What on Earth," Cody said, as Edward and I tried to keep it together. Nias, head in hands, hunched over his bench looking back—either red faced and angry or laughing, I couldn't quite tell.

"Y'all," Cody said. "Look at this shit. What is going on?"

We turned around to find Elfie, out of the engine car now, dancing with pirates in the middle of the street. Then we noticed a swarm of scarf-wearing, jewelry clad pirates sauntering to the middle of the road. Each walked like their knees were about to buckle and their arms danced in the air for either balance or flair.

Elfie grabbed the cord again. *Ding! Ding!*

Another familiar sound, the clunk of car doors followed. Men were starting to approach the train from all angles now, screaming at Elfie and the Americans.

"Lock the door!" Edward yelled. The doors to the golf cart train cars were two feet high with a small golden chain latch on the outside—most likely a child's lock. A small window stuck out of each door to form a three-foot barrier from foot to chest out of each car.

A man with black hair cut straight across his forehead stared into the train cart. This. This is where I'd get kidnapped. Instead, he spat at us and walked back. A lurch forward, and we were moving again, Elfie back in the driver's seat.

"Well, that was quite the treat! I forgot to tell you, but the new *Pirates of the Caribbean* movie is premiering in Paris tonight!" Elfie was bouncing in her seat. "Did you see me, boys? Dancing with Johnny Depp?"

We had no way of communicating back to our conductor.

After blocking the busiest street in the world for over ten minutes, Elfie could do nothing but smile. Free advertising, I guess.

When we got back to Switzerland, we realized with the time change we actually had less than a day left. Cody, Edward, and I went into their family library and hugged. We were ready to go home.

"What's the first thing you're going to do?" I asked.

"I'm gonna use this racket," Cody said. On day two of the trip, he'd spent $300 of his $350 worth of spending money on the same tennis racket that Roger Federer used, since we were in Switzerland and he needed it for JV Tennis. Now he moped, groaned, and grabbed his stomach, complaining that his tummy was empty, sometimes referring to it as his tum-tum.

"I'm gonna eat something," Edward said. "I feel like I've lost 20 pounds."

"I'm gonna take a shower," I said. "I've missed showers and air conditioning."

Nias came in at the end and said that if we'd like to use the shower, his parents decided we can have it for the last night. I grabbed my things and went into the master bedroom. With the window open, I could smell the grass off the air blowing in, swirling around the tiled room. There's something that I've always thought about European grass that I've only experienced in Colorado or Wyoming—it's sweet and nice. It doesn't smell scorched or dried, and it doesn't look like it could hurt you if you laid on it.

I got into the shower and started to decipher the German shampoo from the German conditioner from the German soap from the German herpes cream. I re-read it: herpes cream. *Herpes cream.* Her-pes Crema.

Ah. I think they have herpes, I said to myself. Well, since I was the first one in, I switched the labels on the shampoo and the herpes cream, got out of the shower and found a metal tin of cigarettes on the sink. I lit one, staring out at the mountains and enjoyed what is the closest to a James Bond moment that I'll ever have—sans the sexual assault.

We made it back from the trip unscathed, drunk again on jet lag and the many freedoms of the English language—and because the flight attendant didn't card us. The next crop of foreign exchange students came and went, not at my house, but another's. I was a senior now, and I didn't have time for childish cross-Atlantic cultural games.

I was one of the few people that I knew that had been to Europe. Sure, my friend Tommy's mom was some sort of Argentinian bourgeoisie and he got to go to Buenos Aires every summer which was essentially the Europe of South America, especially after World War II, but not many had been abroad. I'd had European McDonalds now, I'd watched Nias bring European women home to his European parents' home, smoked a European cigarette which I assumed had some THC in it, and I'd clogged a major artery of one of the world's biggest cities.

My mom asked me how big St. Gallen was. We looked it up and it was about seventy thousand people.

"Like Texarkana," she said.

I shook my head to say no. She didn't understand.

"Funny," she said. "He could've ended up anywhere in that exchange program, but his little town's just like ours. His is near Zurich, ours close to Dallas. His, seventy thousand, ours seventy thousand. Oh, look!" she continued, sorting through my camera, chuckling. "They have double quarter pounders with cheese."

I can see my house from here

Waiting outside the sun-stained brick middle school, my mom late to get me as usual, I grabbed the cord holding the American flag to the pole. Something, a hook or clasp, clanged against the pole when I rippled the warm, bristling rope.

It was always hot on the front lawn of the middle school. An awning built a few years later was reserved for the younger grades, so the sixth through eighth graders could sit in either the cafeteria and peer out the tinted windows or perch on their backpacks on the simmering concrete until their ride showed.

I was often the last of my friends meandering around the parking lot. My mom would reel around sometime after the teachers on parking lot duty had retreated inside. They used umbrellas for both shade and rain protection; their long, floral dresses, blue-jean vests, and tennis visors covered every inch of skin while I sat out in a t-shirt and shorts.

A kid named Andre was always waiting, too. I never knew how he got home until one day when my mom, in her bright yellow Volkswagen Beetle and Sonic Drive Thru Diet Coke, asked me what took his mom so long. I didn't know, but I wondered what held mine up. All of my siblings were in either high school or college, and the ones left in town could drive themselves around, and I was the last passenger any of them wanted.

"Tell him to come over here," she said, unbuckling her seatbelt and turning down the air. I yelled at Andre and waved. He ran towards us, his backpack twice the size of his upper body.

"Hey, Mrs. O'Banion," he said, panting up to the car, rubbing the side, "I love your car."

"Oh, thank you, sweetie. It makes people smile," she said. "So, I like it, too." She had a little plastic flower in a vase that came with the car (she was constantly swapping for a natural flower, but it would die, or the water would slosh onto her lap on a tight corner), and she showed it to him. "Hey, where's your mom? I saw you yesterday, too. Do you need a ride?"

He hopped in the car that day and every day for the next four years.

ශ

He'd been in my class since kindergarten. Always in a different homeroom, I'd noticed him in the hallways or P.E., and I had an inkling he was one of the few minorities at the school. There was also a Native American kid whose snacks we started stealing after our Manifest Destiny lesson, the seeds of racism as fertile in history as in the fifth grade.

Before that ride home, I'd never thought about where Andre lived. His house was in Wamba, a strip of road between the city and countryside a little west of the street you took to my house. The nearest place of business was a lopsided carwash. Wamba was a two-mile stretch of clapboard houses the color of jellybeans clinging to the side of the road with no lines of demarcation, fences, or breaks outside of a few cars parked in the weeds of endless beds of scorched grass and swirling dirt.

Andre never let me or my mom inside his blue and off-white house. The front porch screen was ripped but had a fan going on the ceiling. His grandmother, who I only knew by the name Andre's grandmother, sat on the porch from before school till at least after school every day, smoking unfiltered cigarettes and waving as we picked up and dropped off her grandson. Somedays, she was out there with her neighbors and friends playing cards or drinking I don't know what, fanning themselves in the heat.

Andre ran. I can't remember his walk, but I know his run. He'd lean forward like that first day in the parking, perpetually hunched by the weight of an invisible backpack, lunging at the ground, and catching himself before falling. Then he'd scurry from the car to the porch, the porch to the car, the car to the school, and class to class. He ran up the stairs the first time he came to my house. When we got to the top and overlooked the backyard from the upstairs porch, he spread his arms and yelled, "I can see my house from here!"

I didn't get it. There were more pine trees than mosquitoes back there, and his house was at least ten miles away in the opposite direction. I thought maybe it was the line from Titanic, but I didn't know if black people enjoyed Titanic. I still don't.

My mom insisted I bring Andre to friends' houses or sporting events.

He was quick to win over the moms, especially the white ones, but had a more challenging time with their daughters. When we'd talk about girls at a sleepover or in someone's backyard, Andre was always hypothetically matched up or married to one of the black girls in our class, of which there might've been six, and he only had a chance if another black kid, Compton Rob (he was from Long Beach), wasn't interested.

My pre-K daughter came home the other day to tell me she wanted to smooch a boy. I half expected it to be me since she still considers me a boy, but it was a kid named Mohamad (whom she calls MooMoo), a Muslim kid. Progress.

My mom was always doting on Andre, all the moms did, especially with his favorite delicacy: chips. Plain, kettle, sea salt and vinegar, jalapeño, pickle, sour cream and onion, onion, Flamin' Hot, salt and pepper, and barbecue—especially barbecue. She'd often send Andre home with a flat of chips, the ones you get for $10.99 and come with thirty bags. The ones she never bought for my siblings or me but would have, coincidentally, in the yellow Volkswagen Beetle's trunk when dropping off Andre or out when he was over. My mom would ask me what Andre ate for lunch that day, enough to the point that I started asking him to write it down so I could remember. I've recently realized, while observing my own kids' eating habits, that Andre usually only had three or four bags of chips scattered on the lunch table, sometimes trading up for a pudding or sandwich.

For his part, Andre was a good sport. When the middle school dance called for costumes, he and our friend Adam went as the Men in Black, or at least they did for five minutes before Andre stripped off the black tie, glasses, shoes, and socks and sprinted across the gym floor to jump in a picture. He came with me the next year as a black hobbit to circumvent the lost-shoe issue. He'd get looped into Mass some days and was probably better behaved than me. He thanked people for their kindness but never shied from asserting his tastes—he hated lasagna and always politely declined if someone made it. "It's not good," he'd say, shrugging and laughing like the whole concept of cheese, sauce, and noodles was ridiculous.

This won't come across as a particularly contemporary parable about a white kid learning from his temporary black friend. I learned a great deal from Andre. Mostly what it meant to be black in a small southern town when your grandmother is late picking you up from school. And how many chips a human can eat, and what the term "ashy" means. Golem coveted the ring—Andre coveted bottles of Dove. He was always picking at his hair, and if we ever played a video game and you could create your avatar, he made it with cornrows—something that he never had.

Now he's a barber in Texarkana. He displays straight edges and stylish cuts on his Facebook, and I can't help but think, that's art.

My mom updates me on his shop's success after she sees him in Target, which is a regular occurrence for anyone in town—running into my mom in Target. She might sleep on the baby aisle to get a leg up on any pregnancy announcements.

I haven't seen him in over a decade, but I saw on Facebook that he got those cornrows.

We lost touch around high school before he got kicked out our junior year—the rumor was either drugs or a weapon—but our assistant principal got stabbed with a pair of scissors the same year, and that girl got to stay, and another kid overdosed twice, and they let him back in until the drugs finally took, so I was never sold on either story.

My last concrete memory of Andre was my mom pulling up to his house to drop off some food and Christmas presents for his grandmother. One of them was a blue and green 10-speed mountain bike. He'd wanted a BMX bike, but, as my mom explained to both of us, it wasn't practical. We wanted one with pegs on the front and back to make transportation easier, sure, but mainly to see who would chicken out the fastest on some trick we'd seen on TV.

"We live out in the country," she told us. "A road or mountain bike will get you there faster."

When we saw him walking a week later, my mom pulled over and picked him up. He flipped the seat latch of what was now a creaky yellow Volkswagen Beetle like he'd been expecting the ride, and climbed over the seats, talking about a movie he wanted to see. She asked where the bike had gone.

"Pawned. She woudna pawned a BMX bike," he said.

"Well, you can have Casey's," she said. "He needs to run wherever he's going anyway if he's going to lose some weight."

Andre and I laughed, and we kept bouncing over the gravel road towards Adam's house, where Andre would accidentally spoil the end of the Chicago Bulls game before Adam's dad could pop it into the VCR.

He took off, laughing as he sprinted down the street to Wamba.

The Tough Man

The floor of the Four-States Fair Ground stadium was always wet. It never made sense because I'd thought it was for livestock shows in the summers, or at least you could still smell the cleared hay and manure months later—why was it wet? The building looked more like a child's dream fort than an actual stadium—like four football field-sized sheets of corrugated metal walls leaning against another with a plywood roof.

It was the center of an actual fair in the fall—the Fall Four-States Fair—and I know for sure what they used it for in the spring: The Texarkana Tough Man (or Tri-State Tough Man Tournament depending on who you asked. The town was always big on alliteration and leaving Oklahoma out of sponsored events).

The Tough Man was simple on its face, an easy pitch to what I imagine was a receptive chamber of commerce in the 80's: local men box. Sell tickets, sell popcorn, and sell the glory.

I'm not sure if anything in high school held my attention as much as The Tough Man and this includes the assistant cheerleading coach and English student-teacher, Ms. Duke, who I asked to take me to multiple cross country meets under the guise of watching my friends run, in a circle, in the woods, for hours on end.

The Tough Man was a step back in time before I even had a formidable grasp on what time was and where it was going. It's like a good animated movie now—I don't think this is meant for me, but I love it when the clown fish dad finds his clown fish son with the help of the lesbian blue fish with the traumatic brain injury. In a similar yet less ethnically heterogenous, less wet but still damp setting, The Tough Man brought the town together. And in the greatest example of self-reflection and litigious concern, the powers that be made the fights three minutes long, no breaks. So, with the promise of no round two, that meant it was three uncut minutes of furious, out-of-shape, flailing fists and almost exclusively head shots. Nobody had time to test the ribs.

A guy I knew from school, Aaron Durant, was there every year to watch his dad fight. Aaron was pushing what I imagine was four-hundred pounds as a junior, which made him just big enough for a football coach to slobber over, but just slow enough to not make the team. His dad fought in a big blue Carhartt shirt with the sleeves ripped off at the shoulder. The frayed edges shot out around his sagging biceps. It looked wholly dissimilar from the shirts I saw on Spring Break, this one had been ripped by time not vanity.

Mr. Durant's fighting nickname escapes me, but his fighting style never will. He would use his enormous frame—sculpted on the funnel cakes and gator on a stick they sold at the door—to wedge his opponent, a banker, preacher, or factory worker, into the ring's corner, then slam his gloves in an open-palmed slap across their face, one after the other, twisting at his hips with his feet planted to the mat, like he was tossing pizza dough from each glove, before either he or the other man collapsed. He usually lasted between thirty and forty-five seconds.

Our baseball coach took part one year, winning the whole tournament, and, according to multiple sources deep inside the school and the coach himself—the prize was five thousand dollars and the chance to fight a muzzled, de-clawed brown bear. According to Coach Ford—he won that fight, too, and according to court records, another fight years later with his wife. He's undefeated, much like the team he coached the next year.

The Tough Man, unfortunately, moved on with the times. Multiple deaths from 2008-2011 knocked the tournament out of its official capacity at the fair grounds and back into driveways and Waffle Houses around the county.

ɞ

The word tough makes me laugh today. Not rough, not strong, not stubborn, not smart, not powerful… tough. I don't tell my son to stop crying when his sister snatches the Peppa Pig doll out of his hands, or to connect to his inner self when she shoves him to the ground, falling over a sea of Lego bridges he's positioned into a roadblock for the VW Beetle Hot Wheel set I bought for him last year with the full intention of using it all myself. No, I say, *hey, toughen up*! It's a universal concept that fights from adjective to noun to verb and that requires no skill or real training outside of experience to master.

My dad got me a job welding in high school and when I got home from my first day, I told him I hadn't learned anything, but I'd never been that tired in my entire life. "Good," he'd said. "That's the point."

The last time I saw Aaron Durant he'd lost about as much weight as I've gained, and he said his dad is doing great—misses The Tough Man.

On Naming My Son

We scanned all of the baby name books when our daughter was born. Sarah, Willow, Evelyn, Jennifer, Sally, Emily, Sara again but without the h, and Morgan. Melissa, my wife's name, means honeybee or brave, depending on your research.

We chose the name Flannery because it wasn't in the baby book, we didn't quite grasp the monumental task of naming someone for the rest of their lives, and Flanney O'Connor was Catholic, Irish, and from the south—the pasty-skin triple threat my ancestors once dreamt.

We scanned all of the baby name books when our son was coming, too. Wallace was my grandmother's maiden name, on my dad's side, and Wally would be a great nickname. As a little brother, I always wanted to be an older brother, so Wally Cleaver stood out to me more than the Beaver. But I never actually met that grandmother, so it felt a hollow honor at best.

Oscar was my grandfather's first name, on my mom's side, and my wife's maternal grandfather's middle name. The alliteration might be a bit much, but I was teaching at an all-boys Catholic school at the time, and I couldn't imagine a kid introducing himself as *Oscar O'Banion* with a straight face. That was out.

Our parents thought this was all pretty silly. *Just pick a name*, they'd say.

"But this will be his name for forever. He can't change it. Flannery's might change, but his probably won't. This is permanent. Same first name, same middle, same last. It needs to be dignified and unique."

We had certainly convinced ourselves that the monochromatic still photo held by the Cancun magnet on the fridge was going to be some kind of strait-laced accountant. Maybe an attorney like I was supposed to be. But he was definitely not going rogue and hyphenating his last name in thirty years, right? Hell, a friend of mine changed his son's name after a couple of months because their pharmacist couldn't pronounce it. Why they were bringing young Gardner *née* Hayden to the pharmacist so often, escapes me.

"We aren't a dynasty or something," my mom said one day. "Why do you need to name him *after* someone?"

With four months to go, I heard a man on NPR describe how relieved he was when he impregnated his live-in girlfriend so his family line could continue. He was the last male in his family and coming to grips with the lineage dying on his watch hit home as his son was born. "I couldn't be the last one," he said. He named his son Jack if I recall correctly. That's a decent enough heir, I thought, but my boss's son's name was Jack, so how would that look at the Christmas party. That interview gave me a whole new sense of purpose with this name, and the feeling that Terry Gross might've been my middle school librarian. Also, Jack might be the best name a white kid can have: it's unique but not *too* unique, it doesn't have a silly nickname—it's already a nickname of sorts—and there's only one common spelling. Nothing silly like Casey and Kayce, Jeffrey and Geoffrey. But Jack O'Banion wouldn't work because *Jack-O*. Sounds like he's got Tourette's or something. And I have a cousin and nephew named Jack.

My name is registered with the State of Texas as Cason Emile O'Banion, but the IRS knows me by Casey O'Banion, Cason O'Banion, and the always charming, Carson OBanion – add the r, remove the apostrophe. I have three different credit scores to this day, and even I juggle which is in the 700s. All of my past due debt goes directly to Carson. Carson is living a careless life, in my mind. The IRS will get him one day, but he'll go down with a fight.

With this in mind, I told my wife our son had to go by whatever was on the birth certificate. Well acquainted with the burden of the apostrophe at this point, she agreed.

"How about Henry," she said to me with three months left.

"No," I said, "Everyone is naming their son Henry now."

"Because it's a good name," she said.

"I can't have him being the next Cade." While teaching at an all-boys school during the 2018-2019 school year, I had exactly eleven versions of Cade in my classroom. There was the Cade that was quiet and became upset with me for spoiling the new Star Wars movie with an exam bonus question, the Kade that was smart but sandbagged his way into the regular English, and the Cade that I watched take his jacket off one blurry day and hand to an elderly priest. This last Cade would commit suicide a year later. One of the Cade's mom told me she'd never even heard of the name Cade when she named her Cade, Cade. She thought she'd made it up on the spot—Caleb and Wade, she said. But no, I couldn't allow him to be one of twelve on a school roster.

He'll be an individual! Besides, Henry was the eleventh most used boy's name according to the previous year's census numbers.

My wife's maiden name is Lee, but my sister's name is Leigh. We liked the name Jack, but we have two nephews named Jack. Melissa loved my middle name, but I knew that was only priming him for a few awkward years of middle school, which might be the worst time to have a girl's name, and it was the fat rat's name in a Disney movie so that wouldn't work.

My mom's great aunt was Sam Houston's second wife. Sam Houston was the first and third president of Texas, so that's important enough for a school teacher and marketing director's son, we thought. But we lived in Houston for three years and didn't like the sound of it. It reminded me of all the kids I grew up with named Dallas, and I think Sam Houston's second wife might've been his cousin.

My graduating and surrounding classes had a Dallas, Austin, Waco, Tyler, Cody, Cash, Rylan, JaCoby, Doyle, Vann, Silo, Cricket, Buck, Hunter, Farmer, Brittney, Brittany, Britnee, Jessie, Rhett, Donald Keith, John Kyle, and John Travis. No, my son wouldn't carry that torch. Even the formal sounding friends like Sanford Whatley Gay II went by Bo, Beau later in life. Remington Browning Savage III was a class behind me in high school. He sounded like a perfect debutant escort until you realized each one of them is a different gun brand. He got kicked out of school my senior year for having a Browning shotgun in his truck. What if my son's name was Henry came up with something as mind numbing as the next assembly line? If it was a self-fulfilling prophecy I was after, I'd name him Shaq.

So maybe we won't be christening a prince, but we certainly won't be naming him after a town in Texas, I told my wife one day. She didn't see what the big deal was. She grew up seventy-five miles away in a town of three hundred thousand. She had a David, Nick, Ben and Becca to my Cleat, Cheeseburger, Blaze, and Brynleigh.

No, we could do better. We are better.

I sat in the waiting room at the hospital in Baton Rouge, Louisiana in July of 2020. Melissa was getting an epidural, so they asked me to leave the delivery room for a while. The waiting room had tinted long windows that stretched from floor to ceiling. The tint didn't muffle the glare on the T.V. as I watched an episode of *Bar Rescue* on Spike. The show's hot-tempered host screamed at the blank, ghost-white face of a bar owner who had been drinking on the job and ignoring health code violations like his bartender peeing in the trough behind the bar – easy to miss things. When the episode went to commercial, the bar's neon sign slashed across the screen: O'Banion's!

"No fucking way," I said. There was only one other person in the room, a man with thick, wide glasses on. He glanced to me, the T.V., then back to his phone. I mumbled something to get his attention back to the T.V. until I could see I had him.

"Oh, wow," he said. "That's a small world." He looked back at his phone. There was a giant blue wreath on his knee, positioned so his dark jeans were poking through the middle. I how things were going, and he looked up again. Fine, he said, just nervous. I wanted to give some grand advice, but I was only thirty-one, so I didn't think I could.

"What's the name going to be?" I asked.

"Oh, we aren't telling anyone until he's born," he said.

"Like, it's a secret or you don't know?" I said.

"We just aren't telling anyone. It's not a big deal."

I had to know. I asked how they might pull off the name reveal – a banner, social media, or would a plane write it in the sky? Was this kid going to change the world? Why all this secrecy? "You're right, it isn't a big deal. Just tell me."

He got up and left the room, and a few minutes later, I could see him down by the walking path encircling the man-made pond. A few ducks landed later, and I remembered my friend in Baton Rouge's dog died the week before—Goose. Goose was a good name, I thought. No nicknames, I thought. Just Goose.

A nurse broke my concentration when she called me back to the room. The delivery took all of four minutes—two pushes and two sets of heavy breathing and hand squeezing—and here he was. July 29th, 2020—my dad, and a niece and nephew's birthdays.

"What about Dennis?" I said. My dad's name is Dennis David O'Banion, my older brother is Dennis David O'Banion Jr., but he named his son Otis after the elevator brand. Dennis was 782nd most popular in the previous year's census numbers. The census lacked any evidence on Otis' numbers.

"Not Dennis," she said. "But we can use it as a middle name. I like Henry."

I groaned. I pulled out my phone and stared at the names surrounding it on the census—maybe we overlooked something. Ezekiel, Ezra, Elijah, and Noah. We aren't that religious, and had we been, I have a friend named Noah and the letter E looks strange capitalized in a signature, so those were all out.

"We can call him Hank," she said, whipping away sweat and tears, "if you just can't do Henry for whatever reason."

"Like the cow dog?" I asked, fiercely scrolling through my phone for an aberration of insight.

"No, not like the cow dog, Casey," she said, now wincing as the doctor threaded her birth canal back together. "Maybe like Hank Aaron. The football player or whatever."

Hank Aaron I could deal with. "Alright, Henry Dennis it is. We'll call him Hank. Or what about just H.D. like the T.V?" I proceeded to tell her about the serendipitous bar-centered T.V. show in the waiting room as she held Henry or Hank to her chest, his screaming lungs piercing the room and his little feet danced against her stomach. The doctor rated the birth a ten out of ten and said it was the fastest she'd ever seen.

A day later, baby in tow, I rolled my Melissa to our car. She was crying, holding Henry or Hank tight, and thanking the nurses as we stopped to talk to the lactation specialist behind her station. There were rows of balloons and bows, blue or pink, down the hallway. Except for one door. It reminded me of Flannery's birth. We were in a nervous blur for twenty-four hours, rushing to the phone, to the bed, to the bathroom. Then in an instant, a fierce instant of blood and crying, Flannery came. One nurse, who joked about being drunk earlier when she botched the IV placement, took my phone and snapped pictures of Melissa mid-delivery. When she asked the name, I told her and she assumed the road in north Baton Rouge—it was a safe assumption and I didn't have time to explain the complicated past and present of Flannery O'Connor, so I went with it. "Yeah, Flannery Road. It's where she was conceived," which the nurse loved, but she thought I said it's where I'd been *saved*. Either one was fine with me.

That night I sat still in the dark, Melissa still unable to move, as Flannery screamed and screamed, her tongue rattling against her gums like a maraca. A slice of light cut under our door with a series of beeps and squeaking feet from outside, from a world without a bleating baby. And for a moment, I thought about how easy it would be to leave—just go—for a man, that is. My legs still worked. And in the room next to us that night, a woman was alone with her baby, no pomp or circumstance. I'd seen her the day before when she was pacing in the hall and gave us a soft smile while holding her back and belly like she might tip either way. Nobody to share the microwaved broccoli with or help soften the blow to the lactation consultant that you'd be using formula. No visitors, just a bill waiting on her at the end. And in that moment in the dark, I cried for me and that woman. It's a very brave thing, having a kid with someone else, and even braver without.

Melissa tapped me on the hand, and I came back to the buzzing fluorescent hallway. Let's go, I said, and we sped past a door with a huge blue wreath hanging outside. "Kayden" written in lily white string along the top and "Cole" in dark blue on the bottom—"K.C." in the middle.

"Jesus Christ, Melissa. That's what that guy was so worried about?"

Local Flavor

I read an Anthony Bourdain quote the other day: "Food is everything we are. It's an extension of nationalist feeling, ethnic feeling, your personal history, your province, your region, your tribe, *your grandma*. It's inseparable from those from the get-go."

I have to wonder if the late Mr. Bourdain ever had the triple dipper appetizer from the Chili's in Texarkana, Texas next to the mall on a Saturday night before the homecoming dance. It isn't his fault—you can't expect food writers, accomplished chefs, or celebrity cuisine curators to appreciate the delicacy of a fried southwestern eggroll paired with cilantro ranch and a cheeky Dr. Pepper, the dust of a local high school's football jersey hanging above comes floating down to your plate, adding a grainy coating that you didn't know you needed. The girl across from me, her dad out in a leased Suburban in the parking lot, has a flower the size of a watermelon stuck to her dress, and I feel my parents' credit card burning a hole in my pocket, just waiting to be slapped on the tiled table, picking up the tab before I compliment the demi-glace honey mustard sauce on the chicken crispers I'd ordered for the table.

I could've had her dad take us to Texas Roadhouse up the street by the Bass Pro Shop, probably where my dad would rather his money be spent, but the Rattlesnake Bites—their version of a cream cheese stuffed jalapeño—gave me a stomachache last time, and the peanuts on the floor wasn't the atmosphere I wanted to cultivate tonight.

Olive Garden was always an option, but I knew I couldn't resist the Tour of Italy, and nobody wants to dance the night away after the never-ending breadsticks. My friend Brian tried it once our sophomore year and either the fry on the calamari was off or he was predisposed to puking after rapid movements. He ruined a perfectly good Dillard's tie. My friend Cody was working tables at Olive Garden that night and still does as the general and corporate wine acquisitions manager—people that didn't go to school as long as I did are always running around with better jobs than me.

On the subject of seafood—Red Lobster's cheddar biscuits would be the ultimate pairing if things went well enough for me to get to make out later. The garlic-herb flakes of bread hiding between my braces, or hers! *Devine.* But the coconut shrimp were cold last time, and besides, there was a rumor Joe's Crab Shack was coming to town, and I wanted to save room for the grand opening.

On the Boarder is the safe Mexican choice—the more local places don't serve real queso but instead have homemade corn tortillas and this green salsa that goes on everything – no thanks. But On the Border was too close to Texarkana's actual Texas and Arkansas border, no doubt a selling point for the town's restaurant acquisition group but too far a drive for my date's dad tonight. Ta'Molly's was good enough but local.

Our friend Kameron's parents opened up a catfish place down the street, but it lacked the corporate panache and budget, and customers flocked to the chain catfish spot on the Arkansas side with fresh Vietnamese catfish instead.

Another local spot was The Dixie Diner, where I served tables during the summer and got to watch them make the mayonnaise in a bathtub in the back. I couldn't step back on that green carpet until I'd that erased from memory. The owners opened up every morning, their son-in-law, an engineer by trade, managed the high schoolers and dropouts that ran the rolls and salads to each table. I have many less than fond memories of licking the yeast off the bread on hungover mornings during the summer while Jerry, a large man in a slimming black apron, smoked a cigarette out back and told me to "stay off the mess," that night. I probably didn't but lacked a cell phone, so I couldn't call out sick the next morning. They're still going today, probably subsidized by the Sunday service crowd that a fleet of sailors couldn't satisfy—the rest of the days the restaurant sits as empty as the other mom and pop shops around town.

In his review of *Star Wars Episode 1: The Phantom Menace*, Roger Ebert wrote how quickly we are tamed by the extraordinary, our senses muffled by advancement. "I am reminded," he wrote, "of the Isaac Asimov story "Nightfall," about the planet where the stars were visible only once in a thousand years. So awesome was the sight that it drove men mad. We who can see the stars every night glance up casually at the cosmos and then quickly down again, searching for a Dairy Queen." To borrow from Dairy Queen's corporate marketing team, since country music, Dr. Pepper, the 2nd amendment, and horses never quite fit into Texarkana's cultural landscape, I'd have to say DQ is what I like most about Texas. What's a thrill like watching ice cream not succumb a twist of gravity? But no matter—Dairy Queen was for after a football game, not homecoming.

Applebee's too packed, Cheesecake Factory too old money, the Cracker Barrell too quaint, and Benihana a bit much on the senses, I had to find something that screamed *I love you* but without ruining a well-crafted aloofness. The hibachi-sushi restaurant in town was run by the Kim family, and often frequented by the men from the rubber tire factory across town. Sometime before high school, the company relocated much of its tire operation to China, so the dads around town, many of them our Little League coaches or PTA members, spent months or years over there helping train the new workforce. When they came back, they traded in the barbeque for hoisin sauce. The first time I'd try sushi would be with a table of grease-soaked foremen from the tire plant, grabbing and clawing at the spread with their dirty hands like mechanics pulling at a junk yard engine.

Bennigan's. Bennigan's was the answer. With that fare and my last name, I might be able to convince her my family owned it. Alas, it too was out of reach, down the interstate past the airport.

"Your grandma," I mutter today, repeating Bourdain. My grandma, *Ma Mère*, we called her, would scoff at the delicacies on any of these menus. She'd no doubt chide the crispers, throw out the bacon burgers, and giggle at the rattlesnake bites. She'd drone about her hometown and it's cooking.

"It was beautiful. There was a soul to the cooking," she'd say. "There might be better gastronomic destinations, but there is no place more uniquely wonderful. It's vibrant, diverse, and influential. The food was transcendent. There's no place like New Orleans, Casey."

"Right. Okay, Ma Mère," I'd say, "Try the Awesome Blossom with the Ass-Kickin' sauce and see what you say." Did she expect me to go Papadeaux's, that my friend Brian pronounced Papa-Doc's when we were in Dallas one time—almost making my mom die from laughter—did she expect that authenticity? My mom would shake her head at the both of us and tell me to quiet down and that Ma Mère gets confused and emotional sometimes. She was always blaming dementia for things like that, but how much is that really an excuse?

No, this boneless wing basket, this molten chocolate cake, this skillet queso would do just fine. Maybe Mr. Bourdain was right about food being an extension of who we are, but maybe not about the grandma thing.

Pilgrim's Pride

My parents built a lake house on the grassy shoreline of a man-made body of water in a small town near our home in Texas. The town—a four-thousand-person community under the thumb of chicken magnate Bo Pilgrim, who owned the bank, the schools, the newspaper, and a monstrous home in the middle that, according to *Last Week Tonight* on HBO, had a golden bathroom with a nude painting of himself hanging above the toilet. The high school's mascot was even the pilgrims before changing to the pirates, which my brother David would contend are the same.

The lake house—named O'Buoy after an extensive voting process where my pick, The House that Ailing Gallbladders Built, lost in the first round—was complete with shiplap walls and garish water-themed fare. There was a painting of a bloated fish breaching the waves. A wooden bear holding a sign reading HERE LIVES AN OLD BEAR WITH HIS HONEY, and another with WE'RE ON LAKE TIME NOW! My favorite is the wall of family pictures where Butch Cassidy, the Sundance Kid, and Val Kilmer as Doc Holliday make an appearance next to my wedding photo.

I don't know much about Bo Pilgrim besides his silhouette around town with a flat-brimmed quaker hat. There are also multiple statues: him standing triumphantly over the downtown square, him gazing out over the river, and him sitting on a park bench, ready to lend an ear. I've heard there's one of him holding a chicken, too. He was also a significant donor to Jeb Bush's 2016 presidential run. So old Bo might've saved us from quite a bit with a little more chicken scratch on checkbooks.

The lake—dug up and designed by Titus County Fresh Water Supply District President Bob Sandlin during his first and only term—was filled so hastily that the trees it covered hadn't the time to topple over. Instead, they remained upright, creating a network of large nests for bass and crappie to nuzzle into branches like mockingbirds flying through the water. Fishermen loiter over, skimming the top with their quiet troller motors and embracing the shade of the interstate that cuts the lake in two. The snags of the treetops spring out of the water, cutting through an otherwise serene existence and making it a skier's obstacle course, the old ruins of the east Texas forest looming underneath. The lake bends around for a few miles until it seeps into a decaying tire refinery, Bob Sandlin's primary purpose for building the reservoir and the reason he was axed after one year. He named the lake, Lake Bob Sandlin. Not Robert Sandlin Lake, not Sandlin Lake, but Lake Bob Sandlin. Somehow both identifying and crass.

The lake's rocky waters bounce off the concrete storm wall on the peninsula's eastern side near my parents' house. The lots belong to Dallas runoffs and other east Texas residents that have likely miscalculated their proximity to the more inviting colony of Ozark lakes just an hour or two north.

My parents, their lot just to the right of the peninsula's peak, have run off more than a few suitors for the tip's plot, attempting to keep their view of the interstate intact.

A sprawling compound rests against four wooden boat docks along the lake's western side. A helipad and a water-plane runway of buoys bobbing in the wake of a passing jet ski encircle the perimeter. It's the Pilgrim lake house. You can see five or six different structures from your pontoon boat, including a tennis court and a great, grand American flag waving every morning. There's a firework show each Independence Day, Christmas Eve, and New Year's Day.

One of the last times I went, on David's fortieth birthday, we went to see the Pilgrim's fireworks show. Bo, dead and gone, left his family to run it, or maybe some Dallas folk who bought the property. So, we sat in my dad's pontoon with my brother's tennis partner, Jeremiah, and his boyfriend, Coleman. Jeremiah, also creeping up on forty, performed a snippet of his old high school baton twirling routine to "God Bless America" while mortar shells and bottle rockets exploded behind. My dad fiddled with the radio, trying to get his new favorite song, "Gin and Juice" (not the Snoop Dogg version but The Gourds country variety), to play while chatting with Coleman.

"You want to go on the innertube tomorrow, huh, Coleman?"

"Yeah... I haven't been on one in years."

"You ever had a water enema before?" my dad asked, laughing.

"Don't ask," Coleman said, a light flickering in front of his face signaling a drag on some kind of vape pen, "what you don't wanna know."

My dad bent over laughing, shaking his head as a red, white, and blue shell burst over the boat.

Bob and Bo, somewhere in the dirt nearby, might've loved this scene on their water seconds before their explosive American holiday party, but the checks to Jeb Bush and the smoking tire refinery make me think otherwise. Still, east Texas can't help but change eventually.

Aim For Success

There is absolutely nobody on the dusty three-acre playground, nobody on the tennis courts, nobody on the overgrown little league field, and nobody on the searing steel monkey bars. A line of pines encircle the back of Pleasant Grove Middle School, towering over the recess area as the school bell rattles down the tin roof of the breezeway, signaling the onslaught of uncoordinated land rushers to claim their stake of the shade or sun.

Recess in sixth grade coincided with our girls learning that running around with the boys wasn't as fruitful as having them run after you, so they usually grouped up under the shade by the T-buildings (classrooms in trailers that I always assumed the purpose was to punish teachers, but later found out that private schools also use them, usually in between periods of remodeling). Some boys would play wall-ball, clanking tennis balls off the brown linoleum of the T-buildings while class was in session, hitting a plastic window on occasion and drawing the teacher out as kids scattered like bottle rockets.

Sixth grade was also the year before organized middle school football in Texas, so to prepare, we organized similar competitions of our own.

"Smear the queer!" Travis Keller yelled, tossing a warped red kickball at Matthew Maddox. Matthew was an athletic-looking cherub friend who, no matter how tall he got, would never outgrow his head or being short in sixth grade. His head is a watermelon with a sandy blond bowl cut. Travis Keller was one of those kids that got to watch *South Park* in middle school, so he cussed and knew what sex was before any of us got *the talk* from Pleasant Grove Middle School's sanctioned "Aim for Success" program in eighth grade, where they balled up two foil hearts then tried to pull them apart again as stunned onlookers witnessed how wrinkled and torn each seemed after the encounter. I sometimes think of that ball when I'm attempting some new maneuver with my wife.

"Fuck!" Matthew yelled, catching the ball, feet in a dead sprint towards the baseball field's outfield, head sagging behind. He got to watch *Beavis and Butt-head.*

I rounded the side of the chain-link fence, attempting to cut off the ball carrier. I understood running angles well enough from chasing snakes with our lawn mower in the backyard. Matthew lived in my neighborhood and slithered away, arcing away from the fence and back towards center-field where he'd attempt a few jukes and spins we learned playing college football video games.

The hunt lasted no more than forty-five seconds before he hurled the ball over his head, sending it into a deep blue sky like a bridal bouquet – a coward's way out that didn't suffice for Travis Keller, who'd track Matthew down moments later, dragging him to the dirt.

"Shit!" the next target shouted, holding the ball out front in a zombie pose and maneuvering around the crowd. There's a saying in football that some people are fast, but some people are fast *in pads*. Similarly, there's a difference in east Texas between fast kids and those fast *in blue jeans*. Brad Meeks was fast in blue jeans. His scrawny frame barely held them up, so the principal often zip-tied them when his belt lacked the holes. They ballooned out from his hips where his thighs should've been and synched above his ankles where he'd rolled them.

"Come get me, fuckers!" he yelled. He lived with his single mom, who once dated Rick Flair, so there's no telling what he got to watch, and there was no chance of catching Brad, his black hair gelled firmly to his forehead, mixing with the sweat and steam of the afternoon.

We spread out in phalanxes, closing the circle around the sixth-grade jackrabbit until the rallying cry echoed against the chain-link fence.

"Smear the queer!"

A rush, a cloud of dust, and a close line later, we were scrapping in a heap of pubescent aggression and masculinity.

As I rose from the pile, unable to shake the ball from someone's untrimmed nails, I caught a single image through the waves of heat rippling from the concrete porch around the edge of the fifth-grade wing.

A woman with a dark bouffant hairdo hunched in a plastic lime green folding chair. Her left-hand fidgeted with her navy blazer, periodically tugging at her skirt – a professional discomfort I wouldn't understand until teaching in a shirt and tie years later.

A broach on her lapel twinkled in the sun. Her body was leaned out over her crossed, pale-hosed legs, and it looked like she was dusting off her shoe or swatting at a swarm of mosquito hawks.

She shot up, and her back stretched over the top of the small, elementary-sized green chair. Her legs were uncrossed and spread now as she raised her feet in the air, wiggling them like a baby giraffe. The sun, which hadn›t reached her under the shade of the cinderblock classroom wall, hit her broach and danced across my eyes through the curtain of dirt from the fracas below me. She let out a short but gratifying sigh and her body deflated, hunching back down, rocking in place.

Gradually, she drew up her right hand and plugged her mouth with a long, white stick, and her body went from Ritalin-induced shaking to completely limp. Her head and hairdo flopped to one side of her neck in an ungraceful way that made me think she›d died. I›d seen a similar death in what would become a seminal theatrical experience of my young life when Travis Keller played Mercutio in Ms. Cox›s class the year before.

Then her head swayed back into equilibrium and blew out a flowing gray cloud which floated up before dispersing in the wind over the tin roof. Her fingers gripped the cigarette the same as she did the chalk, effortlessly twiddling from knuckle to knuckle, but always business-end straight ahead.

I still remember her exhaustion when I'm on the verge of body slamming one of my own children.

"Daddy," my four-year-old daughter says, hands on her hips, looking wholly disappointed in me for a loud moan. "When you feel like you could roar, take a deep breath and count to four…" It's a cute phrase, I concede, but does little to erase any anger I have that my two-year-old son just used a *potty* word – he wouldn't stop calling the cat a "booty butt."

Years later, I saw her again while I held a fresh, firm pack in my hand, pulling off the thin film of cellophane around the top and pulling the first one from its hiding place. I kicked the lighter on and watched it plume into a little orange flower.

I shoot out the little cloud, a tired old dragon's exhale, swivel quickly before stretching and opening the creaking T-building door I was sure they'd found at a prison auction, stepping back into the blasting window unit air conditioner and staring down a gaggle of struggling summer school students I was supposed to show how our country's civics system worked in one week while they cussed and cracked on one another from behind a computer screen. One I could see was calling his own mother a word I feel more uncomfortable writing than I did *queer* earlier in the story.

"These kids," I text some of my friends, "They use the worst fucking language."

Blue Pill

In ninth grade, my friend Patrick invented a friction-based sidewalk material that powered streetlights from concentrated foot traffic energy. Then junior year, he received a composite zero on his state readiness exam—out of protest for what he deemed to be unfocused, "feckless," math instruction the year before. As Patrick explained from state required remedial math our senior year, "If I hadn't known what I'd known before junior calculus, I might've failed it, so I took out the middleman, which happened to be me."

Patrick would go on to be our valedictorian and give a graduation speech about flipping houses and the *Matrix*—not the red pilled kids you see on YouTube preaching government conspiracies—but the actual movie. If you're like me, you regularly encounter people much smarter than you. I consider it a testament to my own intelligence that I have the wits to know when someone else is operating on level or two above my own. Patrick was in a different league, like me discussing astro-industrial physics with the Unabomber. Patrick would take in what you said, rub his head and scratch his eyes, then either laugh or nod in agreement before taking your point and dissecting it to a muddy core you didn't know it had.

He was a genius, and he was also suspended from a week of school our senior year for his actions during the homecoming pageant.

Nine or ten girls made up our school's homecoming court. They'd pick out a fancy dress from Dillard's, then ask a senior boy to serve as an escort, then the boy would make the run to Dillard's to match the sherbet cream sickle dress swatch to a tie. I made the pilgrimage to the Central Mall the week of the homecoming court bonfire, my mother in tow, where we found Patrick and his mom squeaking across the pale tile flooring of the men's department. Patrick's date was wearing a bright purple sequin dress, and the violet checkerboard tie holding up his Adam's apple tensed as he waved around. His thick, muscular neck twisted in the tie like it was a dog's shock collar.

"This is killing me, mother!" we could hear him across the store. He was always sort of proper in an eccentric, fantastic way that lent itself well to scratching heads and confused glances. He once screamed "How did I do, father?" at his dad from the court of an AAU basketball game after his dad pestered him into air-balling a three-pointer.

My mom made a beeline to his, side stepping racks of youth sport coats like an NFL running back, but one with a bouffant hairdo and bedazzled purse. We talked for a minute while our moms discussed the audacity of the dress colors.

I knew Patrick loved heavy metal, which I never took to outside a few songs he showed us in his game room one day. He loved Iron Maiden, Black Sabbath, and I suspect was the main culprit behind the sophomore year assembly to discuss the amount of Megadeth downloaded on the computer lab's BearShare account—the Baptist youth group leader came, pacing and concerned, to ask what the appeal a song like "Skin O'My Teeth" could have. Patrick later blared it for us in his room while he played World of Warcraft. We'd go over sometimes just to listen to him play World of Warcraft. He'd scream at the screen, clicking faster and harder as the night went on—it sounded like an ant colony inside your head, us in the other room hitting a ping pong ball. One day senior year he came to school with a blank expression on his face and the rumor quickly circulated that he'd deleted his WOW character, a healer named Aurora. When we asked later, he said he'd had an epiphany while he (by he, he meant Aurora) sat in an in-game wedding ceremony for two people in his clan. He'd deleted everything before the digital reception.

Patrick was impulsive but rarely wrong. He was fun in that kind of way.

In the mall that day, I asked if he was going to the CD store afterwards. No, his mom drove him. He was unusually quiet, fidgeting with the tie.

"I just hate all of *this*," he said, "*All* of this!" he motioned to the store with waving arms like an inflatable tube outside a car lot. "Why on Earth are we made to adhere to a dress code because we've been *honored* to walk someone fifteen feet? This is ridiculous. I'm not even going to homecoming with Ashley—she's going with her boyfriend from Arkansas High!"

"Yeah," I said, "Tough break, I guess. Who are you going with?"

"Somebody with a purple dress, I guess. I'll ask around tomorrow."

The night of the bonfire, the escorts all lined up in the back of the

Performing Arts Center, a brick indoor amphitheater built a decade before to house the school's one-act plays, academic ceremonies, and annual Aim for Success-Say No to Sex hip-hop assembly.

The curtains parted a bit so we could see students and families packing the rows. At some point the drama teacher came over to give our marching orders—we would walk to the white taped X in the middle of the stage, wait for our court member's name and credentials to be read aloud, then hand them off to a small plank runway that jutted into the middle of the crowd. They'd do a slight turn and come back, then we, the escort, would walk out and model their Dillard's suit.

"Wait–wait–wait!" It was Patrick at the back of the escort line. "First, we have to dress up, then we have to *escort* a girl, parading her about in front of God and my mother, *then* you're telling us we have to walk out and play patsy for Dillard's?" The exhausted state school system employee that was Mrs. Snyder (the drama club mentor, theater arts teacher, speech and debate class teacher, and Performing Arts Center manager) exhaled and rubbed her forehead.

"This wasn't my idea, Patrick. But just walk out, give a little wave or something."

"I suppose it was just an *honor* to be asked to *escort* you'll say!"

"No, I won't say that. And, by all means, just wave from the X—it doesn't matter to me."

"It's the principle of it to me, Mrs. Snyder. I mean, what are *we* doing?" He started to shout and laugh this last part. This same combination usually resulted in encouragement from his peers and full metal consternation from adults. When he got really revved up—you could hear the pitch in his voice rise and his arms started to almost flap. "Guys—let's not just *do* what they say because it's *them* that's saying it!"

"Patrick," someone said up front, "Tonight isn't about us. Just go with the flow for once, man. Jesus."

"Oh! The *flow*! Oh, I'll go with the flow!"

"It's starting, man," I said, and Patrick began pacing back and forth, shaking his head and slapping his ear as if to knock out any bad ideas he might have.

I turned down the catwalk fifteen minutes later (I did a slightly modified Charleston at the edge of the plank that I'm sure made my mom as stressed as it made my pant's button). Patrick came trudging out from behind the curtain, meeting his date's arms, smiling and waving to the crowd with a flat palmed hand and all teeth showing. His smile was frozen stiff across his face like a needle prick might shatter the whole thing. Both rows of teeth exaggeratively shining as his lips formed a slight snarl.

I hadn't noticed the music to this point in the evening. It was probably some form of Baptist church music, which I assumed everything was to some degree, or wedding white noise. But, for whatever inkling of fate there might be, the song changed to what Mrs. Snyder later referred to as an "electric funky hip hop porn melody," as Patrick walked the plank.

He stopped, pointing his ear at the speakers, then stood motionless. The back of his head looked rigid; his neck again strained as the rest of us peered around the curtain. Someone asked what the hell he was doing, then whoops and hollers emitted from the crowd and someone in the shadowed audience shouted, "Let's go, Patrick!"

It started violently and fast. He reached up around his neck and ripped the tie off in a single motion. The crowd erupted as he slid the tie between his legs, flossing himself while humping midair. "Oh, God," Mrs. Snyder yelled, fidgeting with a headset around her neck, before holding the microphone up and screaming for someone to kill the lights.

He threw the tie into a crowd of ninth graders and ripped his shirt off, the buttons popping loud enough that we could hear their muffled break over the music and the crowd which was now on its feet. I could see Patrick's dad yelling, just like the AAU games before, his mom stiff.

The curtains started to close in around him, but not before he'd kicked off a shoe and twirled his jacket above his head, causing a girl in our class, Chastity Burbee—somewhere in her third trimester—to throw up in her chair.

The principal was out on stage behind the curtain in no time. His claim to fame, outside of leading the county's top academic institution, was tagging Derek Jeter out in the minor leagues in the early 90s. He also took a sophomore Biology book to the nose while breaking up a fight the next month, which I wouldn't accept the gravity of until I broke up a fight between two girls in a public high school in Houston in 2015. They'd been fighting over a boyfriend—the social studies teacher.

Mr. Marshall led Patrick through backstage, Patrick screaming that he was just going with *the flow* before his voice trailed off as a swinging door wobbled shut.

Thus ended the greatest strip tease in Texarkana history—I can only say that because I was too young to enter the Electric Cowboy Dance Club before its sad and unfortunate closing in 2008.

Patrick would go on to accept a scholarship to turn down the entire

Ivy League to attend the University of Arkansas before he left to pursue a football career as a walk on at Division III Henderson State. What makes this last part so notable is that Patrick never played football in middle or high school, when a kid in Texas might. There was a rumor that his dad made him wear pads around the house in ninth grade and might tackle him on the way to dinner to toughen him up. A way to put down the soccer ball and pick up a helmet, but it never took. He left Henderson State and graduated from Texas A&M, maybe. He found God somewhere along the way, and I always assume that sort of thing happens at Texas A&M.

The last time I saw him, he'd recently purchased one of our classmate's parents' old popcorn businesses. He fired them on the second day and turned the Pop 'Pop Shop from a barely brick and mortar into a full-scale manufacturing co-packer and moved operations to Dallas. He ran the Girl Scouts out of town and turned the dance team's annual cookie dough drive into a popcorn event.

Just going with the flow, he told me. "I was born to sell popcorn."

Blue Tarp Forts

Back when I could hold my body weight, me and two friends used to shimmy over a small, muddy creek in our neighborhood and build the future of society with blue tarps and burned-out bottle rockets. The creek was easy to jump, but using the branches to swing to the fallen trunk, rotting inches above the water, clogging beer cans and plastic jugs in the stream, made it seem more like we were roughing it and off limits to the housing development taking shape less than a mile away.

Our neighborhood, the Riverlands, had no natural rivers, but all the streets were named after the Danube, Thames, Nile, Tigres, Volga, Rhone, and Red. We weren't quite in the country and far from the sticks, but outside the city limits enough that when kids turned sixteen, they'd refuse to drive out and pick me up for movies.

In elementary and middle school, me and my friends Matthew and Chance worked long hours on our makeshift Terabithia. We raided nearby construction sites on our bikes, grabbing any plywood, tarp, or bungee cord within reach, and into the thick wood where Danube St. bent out of Thames Rd., we'd emerge in a small clearing and construct. The light of the summer sun or a stolen Maglite's batteries dictated our shifts.

We had different names for our group. The Riverland Raiders turned into the Riverland Marauders after I discovered Harry Potter. Matthew, a basketball-headed kid with a bowl cut and fiery attitude, was more into sports than Chance or me, and he'd imagine us as a basketball, football, or hockey team lineup.

In between picking cicada shells off nearby pine trees, we'd run and hide from the older kids, who mostly had dirt bikes and paintball guns. Outside the city limits meant all of us had high-powered go-karts.

The dirt bike kids, in Pixar terms, were the Sid to our Andy. In our elementary years, we'd cautiously pull out into a street or field, allowing the lawnmower-sized go-kart engine to rumble our brains and eyes, wafting in the fumes of the gasoline. All the while listening for the faint but unceremonious crank of a dirt bike engine before scrambling toward our den of twigs and stolen wood. On snow days, this meant sticking to the sanctuary of paved roads.

They always managed to corner Chance in some way or another. He was a year younger than me, three years younger than the redneck Hells Angels Riverlands branch, and the panic would grow in his eyes each time a sputtering kick came from his go-kart's engine.

Everything was cool if you could get away from their ringleader: Nolan. His signature move was to ride up behind you and kick a shoulder blade or spine with an officially sponsored Fox riding boot. I didn't realize until years later just how athletic this maneuver was—I'd been trying to help my daughter ride a bike without training wheels, leaning over the handlebars and briskly walking while sticking my leg out to stop my son's scooter from hitting a nearby parked car. I thought of Nolan and his pre-pubescent talent. He rode his dirt bike across a pond behind our street one year—skidding across the top for sixty-or-so feet like a stone before slamming into the opposite bank. His green Kawasaki gurgled to the bottom until he dove in and hoisted it on the shore like it was a child's tricycle. Again, I was reminded of these rustic feats of heroism while temporarily drowning in a foam pit at an indoor trampoline park, unable to drag myself out before my two-year old dropped her pants and peed on the rubber mat at the pit's shoreline.

The other dirt bike kids all had an air of mischievous hilarity to them—like they might tickle you if they actually caught you—amusingly popping wheelies or laughing as they encircled a smaller kid but never getting off their bikes. Nolan removed all doubt of playful innocence for me in the fourth grade when I watched him, a sixth grader at that point, slam a kid's head into a locker. It was the first time I'd watched a body crumple. I always suspected him of burning down much of our fort later that year. The melted, gnarled tarp roof twisted in all directions like an aqua-Medusa head, and our bottle rocket stash was thoroughly pilfered. The frayed sections of bungee cords dangled from branches, themselves slightly charred by what looked like the licks of a small flame.

I often wondered if Sid and Andy ever played *together*. They were just next door. Maybe Andy could get Sid to play nice, or maybe Sid would've gotten Andy hooked on his ADHD medicine. Either way, I wouldn't test the theory after the locker and fire incidents. So instead, I spent my time around Nolan rushing and screaming through the pine straw.

Time went by and we woke up as the older kids. Never the dirt bike kids, but older, at least. We'd trade the go-karts in for four-wheelers before the transition to adulthood. Roaring down the Thames, helmet and worry-free, slamming into curbs and culverts, hoping to get some temporary mid-air mental clarity before the handlebars crushed into our sternum. If you could gasp for air, you could do it again. Surprisingly only flipped them a few times to my memory.

As the four-wheeler gauges got bigger, we sped faster and faster beyond the clearing in the woods and the blue tarps.

Matthew moved to South Carolina, then back a couple of years later, and joined Chance and me at Pleasant Grove High School. And Nolan, for his part, was moved to a military school in Georgia.

The blue fort was demolished by an invading subdivision, and the creek diverted into a Texas-shaped fountain in front of a house I pass each time I go home. Fewer beer cans and old milk jugs bob in the water now, but somewhere between the cross-section of city life, country roads, and suburban sprawl, the smeared visqueen of adolescent freedom still smolders.

Walking The Cow

My mom called me a few weeks ago to talk to me about our Thanksgiving plans but started telling me about the neighbors' dog. It was missing. There was a man hunt out looking for the dog over a five-hundred-acre land sprawl east of town, "near the lake where he fishes," she said like I would know.

She was short of breath and the jingle of a dog collar would come through the phone every few seconds before she'd call her dog back to her then pick up the pace again. She'd often call on a walk around the neighborhood. When I was young, she picked out our house phone based on the satellite signal it got the further she walked from the house, and even now she refused to go Bluetooth—striding around the countryside with a cell phone up against her ear.

"Casey – I – am – almost – home… Just – a sec." Her breathing cools a bit before she yells at the dog again, this time the dog's panting drowned out the rattle of the collar.

"Wow, that was a longer walk than I thought. Oh, this is weird… The front door is wide-open. Wide. Open. Well, not wide open, but it definitely wasn't closed. You know how sometimes it looks like the wind might've just blown it open? Maybe I didn't close it all the way. I was probably looking for Daisy and forgot to close it. Not like there's much to take in here anyway if someone wanted to."

My parents live far enough out that they never lock their doors. Our house is in what used to be the country but now might be the epicenter of frontier suburbanism. When I was growing up, you might have to ride a quarter mile to your neighbor's house, and they were all from a different architect. My parents had a red brick two story, each window encased by green shutters, and a row of bulging white columns sitting like teeth, and there was a mid-century modern home across a pond, one giant slanting roof like a half open shoe box with floor to ceiling windows the full way around. There was even a one-story white ranch house with a wrap-around porch built to replicate Jefferson Davis's old home. Now when I go home, I see new builds popping up close enough to Trick-or-Treat without the pine straw covered trailer we needed to haul us around when we were kids. Each new house a stucco copy and paste job, sometimes with a big iron Texas star hanging from the exterior like an oversized sheriff's badge.

My mom walked in the house with me on the phone, continuing her story about the missing dog.

I stopped her. "Mom, should you see if someones there?"

"Well, maybe," she said, either short of breath or short with me for interrupting. "Hello?" she called, her mouth away from the phone. "I don't think a robber, or anyone is going to answer me, so that won't do me any good really. Can you imagine if someone answered and I said '*Oh, sorry! Didn't realize this wasn't my house! I'll be going now!*'"

I could imagine them not responding but waiting. A few days before I'd called my mom to ask her if she knew a murder suspect from Dateline. I'd been watching Dateline for years, but this was the first I'd heard Keith Morrison's smooth baritone mention my "sleepy little city on the edge of the state," as he put it. This kid might've killed a girl he met on a dating app after he'd driven to Dallas to meet with her. The drive the Dallas, for a date, seemed crazy enough to investigate to me, and the officers agreed. My mom didn't know him, but she knew his mom and had seen her in Target a few weeks before. "I think she'd mention if her son was just put away for murder. And she didn't."

Case closed.

But now all I could think about was a person in the house—hiding in the pantry or the laundry chute—waiting for her to finish the phone call before making their move. And now all I could imagine was the last phone call from every Dateline episode. There's always a last phone call. I should tell my mom I love her, I thought. They always regret when they don't say that. I'll tell her. Oh, and I'll tell her how much she's meant to me. And how thankful I am that she's always supported me and believed in me and how much she'll be missed. She'll want her funeral to be somber but not sedated, I'm sure. Not an outright celebration, given the circumstances of her death. Oh, and they always say they wished they'd just kept the person on the phone a little longer and maybe the killer would've changed their mind. I'll keep her on the phone a while.

"Casey—can you hear me? You're not saying anything."

"Oh, yeah, I can hear you. Sorry. Was… thinking about something. At work."

"So anyway, the dogs, Ranger and Rollie, were there when Tim was fishing, then he heard a gunshot, and this wasn't a regular gunshot. Not a typical *boom* or anything, Tim said, it was a loud, drawn out, *cra-KOW* sound. And Tim was in Korea, so he would know the difference, and Evelyn was over with us playing Bunco when Tim called her. Casey, she stood up from the table with her phone glued to her face, ran to the other room, and I could see out of the corner of my eye she just kind of collapsed on the couch. Well, she didn't collapse but bent over, with her hand on her forehead like I've never seen her do. I've only seen her upset a couple of times, and she holds it in very well, not like me, but I could see something was wrong. And your dad got back from taking the four-wheeler up to their house to see if Tim was there and he said he wasn't, and I said I think Evelyn is on the phone with Tim right now. And your dad, he gets so fussy when I know something he doesn't, so he snaps and says, I know Malise, I figured, but he didn't' know…"

My mind checked in on the assailant hiding in the walk-in pantry. They, rightly, probably didn't want to attack while she was on the phone which would alert someone to said attack. But, there they was standing or squatting amongst the tubs of peanut butter and bags of sugar, careful not to hit the pyramid of stacked water cooler jugs in the corner.

"And when Evelyn came back in the room, she just looked like death warmed over. Like Jackie Kennedy or something. They love those dogs, Casey. You know, you've seen them, they're kind of those big curly-haired poodle mixes. Well, Evelyn looks at all of us, your dad is standing on the end of the kitchen, and she says, "Ranger is dead. He has been shot." Just like that. I—was—stunned. We immediately start asking: What? How? Who shot him? Who would shoot a dog? Why? Is Tim okay? Where is Tim? Tim is okay, she said. And Rollie, the other dog, is fine. But there was a gun shot, the one I was telling you about a minute ago, while Tim was fishing and the dogs were in the woods behind him, there was a gunshot and Rollie comes running out of the woods and Tim grabbed Rollie and they went to his car and left."

I am hoping the pantry petty thief is as confused as I am.

"Mom… what?"

"That's what I said," she bursts through the phone. I can hear the ice machine rumbling as pieces crunch and fall into an empty cup. She's about to go into the pantry to get water. Now or never… Never. She opens the door and there's nothing waiting on the other end.

But there's still the linen closet. They must be in there.

"I asked Evelyn if they needed any help, but she said no, Tim was on his way back with Rollie and she needed to leave. Well, I don't know the last time you played Bunco, but you can't just leave a game, it messes it up for everyone. So, I asked if your dad could step in for her. She said she didn't care but sounded annoyed with me for asking but I had to ask. Your dad said they should go to some of those houses out there and start knocking on doors with 500 dollars and say "We wont ask questions, we just want the dog back," and he thinks they'd get the dog back in a few days. He thinks someone out there has it. It's so much land, you people are always shooting or hunting but not dogs. I think Ranger is fine."

I hear her take a breath, and I shoot to ask about Thanksgiving. We needed to know where we're expected or invited that year between mine and Melissa's families.

"So, will y'all be in Texarkana or at the lake for Thanksgiving?"

"We'll be here. Anyway, that was all last week. Right before we left for Denver to go to Jack's wedding. It was so beautiful. I'd never been to Estes Park. It was a small wedding, much, much smaller than his brother's and yours, and I guess all of his cousins' weddings, but that's the way Jack wanted it and it was intimate. You know, we could hear the vows, and they wrote them themselves, and well, Katie was the officiant. And you know how I feel about that, your sister is not ordained but really, they just needed someone to be an organizer, or like a master of ceremonies, so she stepped in, but it wasn't in a church or anything, so she didn't have to go online and get some piece of paper saying God allowed her to do this, which I know you and your brother have done, and I know you know I don't like. Well, Jack's wife, Victoria, is so beautiful. She has an arm tattoo, a sleave, they told me, but Jack just looked so happy. There was no mention of the word G-O-D the entire weekend. And Victoria's family was just different than ours but friendly. Her mom was talkative when I met her but when someone mentioned her sons, two are incarcerated, she didn't want to tell me the story, so we stopped talking. I don't know, I thought that would've been interesting to know but I also get it—I'm practically a stranger—well, not really because I'm Jack's aunt. She *should* know me."

"Hey, mom," I say through the phone while leaning on the refrigerator. I think about the robber in the linen closet or the laundry chute or maybe roving around the entire second floor that my parents don't see unless we're home. Or maybe they've left, sensing the inevitable length of this conversation. But I haven't told her how much I love her or how much she means to me. "Melissa just pulled in with the kids. I need to go."

"Oh, okay. Okay, we'll talk again soon. Love you, bye."

"Mom!" I shout, staring at a magnet on my fridge, one of all of us at Christmas in Atlanta the year before. "I love you and you've meant a lot to me."

"Aw. Well, thanks, Casey. You, too. Is everything okay? Are you dying?"

"I'm not sure. But either way I have to go."

"Okay, we'll talk about who I ran into at Mass next time you call. And I had a question about Thanksgiving. We'll talk."

You can gauge a lot about a person in the south based on how much they talk to their mom. For me, it's once a week, usually through prolonged diatribes over a neighbor, sibling, or sport. I heard on an episode of Dateline a fireman from Oklahoma called his mom upwards of fifteen times a day until he was murdered—she knew he was dead by mid-morning because he hadn't phoned.

Incandescent

"Try it," he said. "You have to."

My brother's eyes, smiling and curious, peered over a pale chip covered by a small blotch of deep, muted red liquid. It was *Crazy Asshole Hot Sauce*, from a Firehouse Subs in Texarkana. Firehouse Subs last a few years in town—a firefighter-themed sandwich restaurant that promoted subs like the Hook and Ladder—which was the average lifespan for any area restaurant not named Chili's.

I took a bite, making sure to avoid my lips and the roof of my mouth, then slowly began to cough and slurp a Diet Coke. My brother, David, was coughing too, but from a fit of laughter. We each picked a hot sauce from the gallery of different bottles Firehouse had—each with a different heat rating. I grabbed a nine, I thought out of ten, called *Satan's Toe Jam*. Most of them had ass-themed names or logos like *Butt Twister, Ass in Hell, Ass in the Tub, Rectal Rocket,* and *Ass-pocalypse*. Years later while working in south Louisiana, I met a man peddling a hot sauce, *Swamp Dragon*, that used different liquors as a base over vinegar. It helped with the flavor profiles and shelf life, and it was FDA approved – and great on Bloody Marys. But there's something in a name—*Ass-pocalypse* by any other name wouldn't taste just as hot.

Satan's Toe Jam sounded hot enough. I put it on his salt and vinegar chip and watched as he squirmed, his balding head sweating a little while he clinched his eyes and dunked his tongue into a cup of ice water.

Crazy Asshole Hot Sauce was somehow rated a twelve out of ten on the Firehouse Subs Corporate Scoville scale. My head, also balding, didn't sweat as much as turn beet red and swell, and my eyes immediately watered as I exhaled, my seared breath like a hair dryer.

"Would you two cut it out," my mom said. She was sitting next to me, glancing around the fluorescent lit dining room to see if she knew anyone. "Eat your sandwiches then we'll go get some new shoes."

The place was packed with Texarkana—high school kids working the counter, shouting sandwich orders as adults from the Texas and Arkansas sides milled about, reading the new restaurant's menu before almost assuredly settling on the turkey and ham. We'd said hello to a number of former teachers out on summer break, my dad's attorney whose kids I grew up with and were, according to him, doing well, and my former DARE officer who hadn't spoken to me since seeing me drunk at a college football game four years before.

My old youth soccer coach stopped by the table, Mr. Mulberry. A round but muscular man, Mr. Mulberry was built like a sturdy mushroom. He ran a tight ship on the Bombers during a prolific run our fourth and fifth grade years when his son George, a similar voluminous fungi-shaped boy my age, was our goalkeeper. My brother was taking his daughter to the senior prom that same year, so not much had changed at the table besides my body and their hair density.

His navy suit hugged his arms, gripping his thick shoulders before loosening around the elbow, and his maroon tie loosened as we spoke. I never knew what Mr. Mulberry did—I knew it involved suits, but other than that I was lost. Business, I told myself. Must've majored in accounting, or business, or management, or something, I wonder today. Maybe he was pre-med to business like my roommate in college. Whatever he was, he was nice—always asking how I was or checking in on my progress in JV sports. His eyes performed an abbreviated squint when he smiled, something like a half-drunk smirk. I'd call him lumbering but that implies more goofiness than sheer joy, and Mr. Mulberry was neither. He was perhaps the kindest person whose interactions with me mainly consisted of shouting—usually from a sideline—and watching me gasp for air mid-sprint. In that way I was always confusingly intimidated yet pleasantly surprised to see him, like ordering an omelet and figuring out the place only has crepes.

"So, what've you been up to, Casey?" he asked.

My tongue beginning to blister, I tried speaking without hitting any teeth. "Law school." I could tell this response annoyed my mom.

"He's being goofy. He's in law school, Mike," she said.

"Well, isn't that great—you know George is in med school, right? Well, close to it at least. David, you're a doctor?"

David nodded. "Finishing up a fellowship in Oklahoma City."

"Mike, tell Casey about what you just did—he might be interested. Casey, listen to Mr. Mulberry."

Mr. Mulberry laughed before bending over the table, putting one hand on the gray linoleum top. "So, I was in my hotel room in Austin a couple of months ago—"

"Mike is a state representative now—I'm sure I've told y'all that," my mom said.

"Oh, yeah," he nodded, "I ran last year and was down in Austin for a meeting and just noticed in my room that I couldn't even see my damn notes I'd taken. Right in front of my face, couldn't see them!" He held a napkin and put it on the tip of his nose. "So, I'm like this in my hotel room, and I'm wondering, what is going on here? What's wrong with this picture?"

"And" my mom said, grabbing my arm, "it was the light bulbs."

"The light bulbs," Mr. Mulberry said. "The yellow fluorescent bulbs that were in the lamps of the room weren't strong enough. And I know they're technically better for the environment," he said this last part while waving his hands around the room as if to illustrate, "but a light bulb should emit… light, right? And I couldn't see."

"So, he proposed a bill that the governor signed."

"Yep," he said. "Now Texas is one of the only states that has a choice in their bulbs. And it brought jobs—before they were only making the fluorescent ones in China. Now we can make incandescent ones in Texas and you can choose what you want."

"I think," my brother said. I could see him pausing but also studying Mr. Mulberry's red tie and making connections. "I think that's great, but some people are more worried about whether there will be a planet here in a few centuries rather than which bulb they can use."

Mr. Mulberry didn't miss a beat. "Well, David, I hear your point but there's mercury in fluorescent bulbs, and that's not good for the environment I don't think."

"Oh, the mercury in fluorescent bulbs isn't harmful."

"Well, what about me not being able to see?"

"That'd be like saying you want freedom of choice to wear a seatbelt. You aren't hurting anyone else by not wearing one… until you crash, fly through the windshield and everyone is paying your ambulance and hospital bills, if you're lucky enough to need them."

"Well, I just think it's cool that someone from Texarkana got a bill signed by the *governor* of Texas," my mom said. She'd dropped her sandwich back into the plastic basket and was drinking tea out of the FDNY 9/11 commemorative cup. "Anyway, how's Jenny?"

After Mr. Mulberry left, swinging his sandwich bag back and forth through the jingling door, my mom turned to David. "Why do you have to be like that? It *is* hard to see with those bulbs sometimes."

"It's not about the bulbs," David said, "it's about doing something that's directly impacting the future in such a negative way but waving the flag of freedom as the reason. The minute something meaningful is passed to try and do anything responsible, someone comes along and says, 'But what about me?!' and fucks it up for the rest of us."

My mom cocked her head. Her lips pursed as she shook her head. "We've already spoken about your language, and besides that, I don't see why you can't just be happy about someone you know making an impact. Or why do you have to say something *every time* you don't agree with someone?"

It was a good question. I was in law school and on the verge of identifying my political ideology, and I liked the planet but enjoyed sight as well. But my brother being so passionately on one side of the aisle gave me the natural inclination to join the other. But Mr. Mulberry, being my former soccer coach, made me run more than probably anyone in my life, so I had that to ponder as well.

"I don't always open my mouth, mom. Take Casey, for instance. I watched him order a twelve-inch sandwich on white bread, probably processed to hell, and didn't say a word."

I laughed and took an exaggerated bite of the Hook and Ladder sandwich, finding a pool of *Volc-Anal* sauce, that David had snuck in during the conversation, gushing against my lips and gums. David erupted as I spit the wet lettuce and meat out like a runaway hose.

"Y'all are going to hurt yourselves if you don't cut this out," my mom said, shaking her head and finishing her tea.

A Southern Engagement

We had two engagement parties before our summer wedding in 2016. One in Shreveport, Louisiana where my wife is from—the other in Texarkana. Only seventy miles of unmanicured highway and a few hundred thousand people separated the two at the time (that, and Shreveport had the Bass Pro Shop Texarkana wanted), but the crow's flight revealed a major difference.

Sure, Shreveport's water was undrinkable through significant swaths of the year and blight sprinkled the landscape like their drive thru daiquiri shops, but Shreveport had a PGA tour pro, tennis champions, and a few big-time ambulance attorneys whose jingles made it onto Texarkana's radio.

Our Shreveport party had an invitation with handwritten calligraphy—one of the words being *soiree.*

Our Texarkana party had at least two words written in a font that included a lasso rope—one of the words being *fiesta.*

Shreveport had *horderves*, martinis, and pastel suits. The hosts, who I met that night, gave a toast that included our names, our love, and a blessing for years of happiness and honesty. The house was a giant white plantation-style home with white columns and shrubbery growing at all ends.

Texarkana included multiple keg stands, a margarita mixer churning loudly in the corner, and blue jeans. The hosts, who I'd known most of my life, didn't toast but let a friend's mom scream, "These are your people!" at me while they forced us to unwrap gifts in front of the party. The party was mostly outdoors.

A few southern writers describe southern towns, like Shreveport, with a certain mystic warmth. The rundown casinos, cracked roads, and defunct school systems a shiny penny in the loafer of nostalgia. One writer recently said of a deceased Chinese restaurant owner in Shreveport, "We will miss him always and think of him whenever a great bottle of wine is opened, or a plate of food is shared, or a sacred room is filled with the spirit of friends present and departed."

The restaurant is attached to a motel.

Without speaking ill of the dead or any Asian cuisine, the exalted reverence of stalwart customs in the south breeds the mythical realism injected into their traditions like a motel restaurant, a gas station pie filled with meat, or a debutant ball.

Nobody writes about Texarkana with such hushed respect. Our Chinese restaurants close with little pomp and circumstance, if we had one at all. The closer you get to Texarkana, the more dead armadillos you'll see on the side of the highway. Once you smell a dead skunk, you'd made it.

What the Texarkana party did have was change. William Jean, a childhood friend that I hadn't seen in years but still lived in the neighborhood, stopped by and completed multiple minute-long keg stands. He and his brother went by William and Charles, not Willie and Chuck or Billy and Charlie—William and Charles. So, there was a bit of class. The hosts' son told my dad he wanted to be a monk or a shaman that night and shaved his head. Our Shreveport friends smoked cigars with my high school friend that had Dale Earnhardt Jr's NASCAR number tattooed on his ass.

CASON E. O'BANION is an award-winning writer living with his family in Baton Rouge, Louisiana. His debut novel, *Chinese New Year,* was nominated for the Thurber Prize for American Humor and was a featured novel at the 2024 Louisiana Book Festival. O'Banion's essays about east Texas, chain restaurants, and his family and friends can be found in publications like *The Southern Review, The Dead Mule Literary Journal, The Hyacinth Review,* and more across the internet. O'Banion got his MFA from Antioch and USC in Los Angeles, and a bachelor's and JD from LSU, where he currently teaches writing at the undergraduate level.

www.ingramcontent.com/pod-product-compliance
Lightning Source LLC
Chambersburg PA
CBHW050144110726
47898CB00008B/2667

* 9 7 8 1 6 2 2 8 8 2 9 2 2 *